GOING BACK TO CHURCH

THIS IS MY STORY

R. George Riggon

Going Back To Church: This is My Story

Authored by R.George Riggon.

Copyright: © R.George Riggon 2023

Published by Marcia M Spence of Marcia M Publishing House Ltd. On behalf of R.George Riggon In West Bromwich, West Midlands the UNITED KINGDOM B71.

All rights reserved 2023 R.George Riggon

R.George Riggon asserts the moral right to be identified as the author of this work. The opinions expressed in this published work are those of the author and do not reflect the opinions of Marcia M Publishing House or its editorial team.

This book is sold subject to the conditions it is not, by way of trade or otherwise, lent, hired out or otherwise circulated in any form of binding or cover other than that in which it is published. No part of this publication may be reproduced, stored in a retrieval system or transmitted in any form or by any means (electronic, mechanical, photocopying, recording or otherwise) without prior written permission from the Author or Publisher.

A copy of this publication is legally deposited in The British Library.

ISBN

CONTENTS

Dedication 5

Acknowledgement 7

The Purpose Of This Book 9

Commendation 18

Chapter One: *Life Begins as A Blank Page* 21

Chapter Two: *Unseen Things* 28

Chapter Three: *First Test of Human Free Will* 38

Chapter Four: *A Tropical Childhood* 44

Chapter Five: *A Place of Worship* 52

Chapter Six: *Gathering The Church* 63

Chapter Seven: *A Pentecostal Christian Upbringing* 71

Chapter Eight: *Train The Child* 78

Chapter Nine: *Childhood Baptism* 95

Chapter Ten: *Church Membership* 102

Chapter Eleven: *A Church In The Mother Country* 108

Chapter Twelve: *One Congregation Becomes Three Churches* 115

Chapter Thirteen: *A World of Sports* 124

Chapter Fourteen: *A Time For Renewal* 131

Chapter Fifteen: *Lusts and Desires In The Flesh* 137

Chapter Sixteen: *A Change of Position And Place* 141

Chapter Seventeen: *Going Back to My Childhood Church* 148

Chapter Eighteen: *Confessing Jesus Christ As Personal Saviour And Lord* 153

Chapter Nineteen: *Re-Baptized In Water* 163

Chapter Twenty: *A New Birth of The Spirit* 169

Chapter Twenty-One: *Restored to Christian Fellowship* 184

Chapter Twenty-Two: *Bringing Flesh Under Holy Spirit Control* 191

Chapter Twenty-Three: *Feeding The Spirit* 195

Chapter Twenty-Four: *Worldly Forces Against The Church* 205

Chapter Twenty-Five: *No Turning Back Into The World* 211

About The Author 222

DEDICATION

This book is dedicated to the loving memory of my dearly departed mother, Sybil Eliza Patterson, born in Brownsville, Cascade, Hanover, Jamaica, 100 years ago, on July 27, 1923. May her eternal soul be secured in the rest that is Jesus Christ, unto God the Father. I dedicate this work also to my Sister in Christ, Mrs Joan 'Patsy' Evans-Blake, a past Sunday School teacher at the New Testament Church of God, Mount Pelier District, Sandy Bay, Hanover, Jamaica, who wetted my appetite to learn more about Jesus. Today, I continue to hold in my memory her caring and patient handling of our large class of primary aged children every Sunday morning. That caring nature would get all of us to sit attentively, for at least short spells, and listen to stories about Jesus, Moses, Joseph, Jacob, Daniel and other characters from the Bible. Sister Patsy got me interested in seeking to understand the written words on the pages of the Bible, and though I would fall away from the narrow Christian pathway later in life, I never lost the memory of her encouragement that we must try to behave more like Jesus when we grew up. I give thanks to God for placing both of these wonderful women in the path of my life at such an early stage.

Acknowledgement

The planning, researching, drafting and completion of any book takes time. In the process, one person can only do so much, consuming physical and mental energy, emotion, materials and so forth. The work can get very heavy and the path long and seemingly never ending. But with other good people around, this labour of love became a reality, and I must acknowledge the great support and encouragement by my wife, and sister in the faith, Novelet Hill-Riggon. She sacrificed many long hours to type up the first draft of this work. I thank her for the full and complete interest given for the cause of preparing this final version of my story.

I must also acknowledge the different levels and areas of support and encouragement received from several other persons during the course of planning, drafting and completion. In some cases, the input was direct while at other times, indirectly so. They provided great insight with often few words, and not even knowing this at times. There were others who contributed much by just simply being themselves, so that from things they said quite naturally new thoughts would be triggered to move the work forward. On this Christian journey we are encouraged to rely upon faith, meaning to have a total dependence upon God to lead us through.

I must give thanks to God for placing me among the congregation of the New Testament Church of God at Mount Pelier, for I have come to acknowledge that all things work together for good to those who love the Lord and who are called according to his purpose. We must all be united together in the Christian faith and play our part to promote a greater desire for God, in our families, community and beyond. Let us therefore hope that the echoes of this story will reach out to the attentive ears of others who do not yet know the love and peace of the Lord. May the God of all grace continue to bless and keep us, in the name of Jesus Christ, our Saviour and Lord.

The Purpose Of This Book

※✦✦✦※

It has been the practice of a lifetime for me to gladly exclaim to myself each morning as I awake, 'Thank you God, I am alive another day!' This first moment of consciousness in being alive has to be ranked as the most wonderful feelings that any person can experience each day. Life is our most precious possession and as I stir out of deep sleep and settle into full consciousness each new day, I feel thankful. As a child my mother made it clear to me that God actually exist and is the creator and ruler over all things, from the deepest part of the ocean to the highest heaven. She described God in a way that caused me to picture a great big and powerful force without visible form, having no face or human body. It had always puzzled me that without having eyes He could see, and without legs, God could move, and without hands, He could touch! In the mind of a child, God was like a magnet with force to move visible things at will. I am sure that my mother did not expect that I would understand at my young age and stage, all of the complications and details of just who the God who spoke on the pages of her old King James edition of the Bible was all about. I believe though that my mother was teaching me that although I couldn't see God, in the way that I could see her, I must never doubt the truth of His existence. In time, I would come to find that this very issue was one that occupied the thoughts of many other persons also, at some point in their life. Much of what we believe comes from within immediate social circles of family and friends. Such circles continue to expand quite naturally and continuously throughout our formal schooling, training and working days. I believe God knows the thoughts of every heart and He will continue to provoke us to think about Him every single day, even when we don't want to do so. I also believe my mother when she said that in time, there would be ample opportunities for me to seek after a personal knowledge of just who is our great big, wonderful God.

At the various phases and stages of a lifetime I believe that most people will develop some level of curious thoughts around the starting point or inception of their very being. Such often repeated questions of just who we are do pop up quite naturally in the mind. None of us can avoid giving some thought to the cycle which takes us from birth, through physical growth and development, maturing, and ageing unto death. It is a natural biological cycle that no one can alter and so I think these are things we should all want to know, and not least to get answers to questions of life's purpose, destiny and legacies. These are things of deep interest to us that God already knew in eternity, even as He begun to set in motion streams for creation, reproduction, sustaining and ending life. He caused every human being to become aware of His supreme presence above us and to understand just who we are under His sun and sky. Hence, God has made this possible by giving us the first and most trustworthy written record of divine revelations and illuminations about Himself. For our benefit, we have each received a personal endowment of generous gifts to help us to come to know the truth of God and to apply wisdom in answering life's many questions. I take a great deal of interest in those first five words of the opening chapter of the King James' English translated Bible that say: *'In the beginning God created...'* Hence I have never believed that in the beginning there was a random surge of natural movements, atomic explosions or collisions that can explain, without a responsible doubt, the establishment of every form of life in all the universe. I believe completely that the most accomplished earth scientists, biologists or naturalists have been gifted with wonderful abilities by God, to investigate and explore some of the many secrets hidden in this universe. While it is the pleasure of God to conceal many things it is to our honour that we will begin to search out these things. But there should be no one, under the sun, who should think to challenge or reject the truth of God's sacred holy Word. We can discover only the tip of the iceberg, as it were, for God alone knows the full depth and breadth of His creation.

On the pages of the Bible, only God alone could have revealed the many things about Himself as an eternal Spirit and the possessor of a divine nature for loving kindness. We learn also about our likeness in a moral sense to the character of our creator and which we could never unearth through our own scientific methods. God chose to use persons and things to display the irrefutable evidence of His sovereignty and it is through the giving of the Bible that we have come to know and understand many mysteries of the global earth we inhabit. All this complex expanse is held in perfect balance each day by that great, big, powerful and eternally wonderful God. He alone is the author of both visible things that the eyes can see and also the invisible things that we have not seen.

I was born into a large Jamaican family and came to believe in God from an early age and began to understand the direct connection between sacred and natural things. From earliest days I developed a clear understanding that it is God who established and heads every family and as such the love, care, protection found within us comes from the nature and likeness that He chose to share with us. I am also aware that during my formative years many social and cultural trends started in the previous roaring and swinging decades of 1950s and 60s would later come home to roost. Those were times to explore changes to body, soul and spirit, when many beliefs and familiar practices simply passed away like outdated calendars. In such an atmosphere for change, the very reality of God and of His holiness would face serious and severe challenges from areas of the world that previously promoted them! The Romans became more secular, the Greeks more religious; the British became more home-facing and the Americans more pioneering in establishing churches around the globe. As a child in times of such universal changes, the sounds of gospel music and expression of cultures would also enter my small world. I came to understand some of the clashes between worldly cultural values and the Christian beliefs proclaimed through churches. In my young mind some things would become the anchor, as it were, for where I would come to stand as the years went by and the inevitable storms of life stirs and blows harder and stronger against me. For the most part, it turned out that the early years for me would be quite calm. It was at the end of my primary school years that my foundation stones would be first tested. I had lived with only my mother up to this time. She had left my father in England, and they remained separated. But then almost suddenly she announced that we would be going to live in England with my father! It wasn't long before we were all together as a modern nuclear family. There would then follow a raft of accompanying changes in my life and my foundation stone would begin to move again. There was no uncertainty about who I was and even who God was to me, but the previous instant answers to these very questions became more hesitant in my conscious daily thoughts. On many mornings that I awake I didn't always exclaim the same words of thanks to God for His great mercy and love. This was the beginning of my backsliding. Yet I had not realised that I was drifting away from my earlier talks with God. This was so, I believe, because the devil was allowed to tempt and try me. That old serpent, the tempter from the beginning of human inhabitation of this global earth, had cast a veil over me. As a young teen in the middle of England, I confess that just about everything that I had clung to at my foundation, quickly melted away. Many things that I believed to have been holy or sacred now seemed to be of the world. The winds of change were blowing, and they pretty much moved me to a different place. The devil had cleverly enticed my eyes and ensnared me in his net. I rebelled and was disobedient against the ways and truth of God. I liken the devil's working to an evil paramilitary leader who actively recruits vulnerable and innocent children as soldiers, against their knowledge of his true intentions. Once taken in, it becomes very difficult for the captive child to get out again. Such is the guile of the devil, an active and cunning adversary against the Word and truth of God.

I managed to escape from the devil's grip and today, I want to share my story and give thanks to God for the strength and courage given to allow me to see again in the newness of life. Yet I know that there are countless others who remain ensnared in the same place of darkness where I had been, and they have not yet found a way out. I want to encourage those who remain in bondage to the devil that while it seems to be almost impossible to escape, God can make a way for you to get out. All things are possible with God, if we only believe His faithful and true promises. He will neither leave nor forsake us when we learn to lean and depend on Jesus Christ. One of the expressions which I had often heard my mother repeat, no doubt for my learning, was that a drowning man will clutch at a straw, but he will not cry out for help until he accepts that he is heading into dire strait. There is a present danger in every crisis. The person under the veil of the devil's stronghold may not even notice the severity of their present situation let alone to raise an alarm or to shout out for help. In my case, it had finally dawned upon me that I was at the wrong place and drifting further away into deep water, with my very life at stake. I didn't open my mouth to make the plea or cry out for help. But God is good and He alone knows our heart and even our innermost thoughts.

We don't even have to open our mouths for God to hear our cries. My longing to escape from the devil's stronghold began with a simple prayer which I said in my head repeatedly. I believed that God will not turn away those who earnestly seek after Him, and so I would simply utter:

> *'Father God, I am aware today that I am standing at the wrong place and under the influence of the wrong spirit. I know it is the wrong place because I do not feel comfortable in myself or with my life. I do not feel your presence. I just want to escape from here. Please help me, in Jesus name.'*

Amen.

Today I feel liberated and redeemed by the precious atoning blood of Jesus Christ and walking in the newness of life with a clear purpose and a clear conscience. God is truly good, and I want to tell others about Him. It is for that reason and also, in order to help others to realise that while anyone can be knocked down by the devil, life doesn't have to end just because you are down. Because going down does not amount to you being knocked out from God's loving kindness and mercy. Neither have you been rejected by God. I got away from the devil's strong grip eventually, but I know that many people have not yet escaped. As I reflect today on just where I have been and the dark paths that I might have continued along, I must give thanks to God. This is a personal story of escape to a newness of life, before it was too late. My hope today is that others will also recognize just where they are standing, in relation to the presence of God, and can take courage in the knowledge that all is not yet lost. You are still alive today and have another opportunity to look into the mirror of God's love and ask the only begotten Son, Jesus Christ, to free or liberate you, so that you too will become renewed to fulfil the purpose that God has already set over your precious life.

To God be all glory, honour and praise.

Commendation

✦✦✦

Rev. Glasford Hume

I was actually given the privilege by the host pastor at the Mount Pelier New Testament Church of God, Rev. Oniel Haughton, to administer what turned out to be the second time of water baptism for brother Riggon and his wife, Sister Novelet, during 2016. Today, I warmly welcome this personal testimony from my brother, in the Family of God, and sincerely hope that this book will be a blessing to Christians everywhere. The deep early childhood consciousness of God's presence and sovereign authority over his life has been very illuminating. Thereafter, his personal encounters and struggles to overcome the enemy to our eternal salvation, would begin. This brother was thrown from the path of righteousness before he could begin to grow and better understand the things of God. But in spite of the years of being held captive to sin he did not lose consciousness of the eternal love and grace of the Lord God Almighty. After many years living in England, and away from any church, the brother recognised his state of helplessness without Jesus Christ and cried out, in confession and repentance. The Lord heard and answered him, and by the saving power of the Holy Spirit, he was cut free to resume on the Christian walk. Brother Riggon re-baptized and turned to fellowship at his childhood church and throughout this moving testimony, he has clearly become a committed worker in the vineyard of the Lord at the New Testament Church of God.

On a final note, I am personally very pleased to see the references made to acknowledge the place in history due to the Claremont New Testament Church of God, in Hanover. This church was planted through the tireless labour of a remarkable servant of the Lord, known to us as, 'Brother Bailey', and who hailed from the parish of Clarendon. He settled in the community of Jericho/Claremont in 1937. I welcome this historic record for the New Testament churches in the often-overlooked parish of Hanover.

May the Lord continue to bless and sustain you with every physical and spiritual blessing, my brother.

To God be the glory.

Rev. Glasford Hume – Present pastor at the Haddo New Testament Church of God, Cave District of Churches, Westmoreland, Jamaica. (Former pastor at the Elgin Town, Mount Peace and Claremont New Testament churches, Sandy Bay District of Churches, Hanover, Jamaica).

GOING BACK TO CHURCH

THIS IS MY STORY

R. George Riggon

Chapter One
Life Begins as A Blank Page

The population of this global earth is now estimated to be over seven and a half billion people. This number represents a lot of human beings, spread out across the four corners of the earth and including small clans, large tribes, great nations and continents. Our ordinance maps confirm the sheer vastness of land space and seas. As a child I often thought it incredible that every grown person in the world had been the same small size and age as I was. Each had a mother and a father, just like I did, and who would teach them how to behave during playtime and how to rest and pray before going to sleep at night. It was my mother who confirmed for me that every grown man had once been a new born baby, and so started from the same biological point. In the same breadth she would add that each would also eventually end up at another similar ending point, in death. That would prompt me to enquire further about whatever happened in between those starting and ending points? The answer she illustrated using a piece of blank paper, and that would straighten out my childish reasoning. The start of each child's life was similar in terms of physical size, dependence for shelter, food, water, clothing and warmth.

The mind was also similarly blank at that earliest stage. She likened this stage of life to the description of a piece of blank paper. Her point was that each of us started out with nothing in mind at that first stage. But like the starting of a book, from an initial blank page would later become filled with page after page. There were no marks or characters entered on the page at birth. But over time, that blank page would begin to be filled up with all sorts of marks and characters, images, words and meanings. As one page was filled up a new one would be added. As more years passed the number of pages just increased to become like the book of a person's life, from its blank start to the often complicated ending. Some pages would later bear a record of fear, dread and sorrows; others of joy and gladness. Yet others record confusion and indecision. It is a truth that not everyone born will even get the opportunity to begin to fill up pages. A portion will not live beyond the day of their birth, or got too far into infancy or beyond their early childhood. But for the clear majority of births around the globe some initial entry would have been made and so represent a great number of pages to show at least an initial entry of a life, and leads to a further question of just what should be entered on our pages? In the words of divinely wise king of ancient Israel, Solomon, a life is not given to simply mark an entry on a blank page and then grow and eventually die. King Solomon insisted that for every life there is always a purpose determined, in advance, by God. My mother would certainly agree with this conclusion reached by king Solomon. This was because she believed firmly in the supremacy of God, as author and creator of all things upon the face of the earth. The Holy Bible was one of few books in our house. As a child I came to believe this to be a very sacred and special book. It was a book with many pages and the only book that was opened weekly, with some verses read out aloud. The pages of one book can certainly be used to influence the pages written in another.

The name of king Solomon featured on several pages of the Holy Bible, and as a man who possessed wisdom, knowledge and understanding beyond any other that ever lived, his insisting that while every life opened as a blank page, a clear purpose had already been divinely set for its course. So then in order to fulfil that purpose every person must seek out the course set for their life. So the names of king Solomon, and of his father, king David, entered into my consciousness along with those of Adam and Eve, at a very early stage. It is those conscious thoughts and actions that occupy the entry made on each page completed over a lifetime, and one of these will always drive the other. The things that we become aware of will occupy our thoughts and in turn, they will influence what we choose to do and say as we go through each day of life. So Bible names were prominent in the first book I ever opened. My mother also re-enforced the reality of these as being actual persons. They had lived on this earth a very long time ago. I am inclined to believe that perhaps most children would have heard these names, irrespective of their language, culture or location on the globe.

The pages that filled the lives of these persons were made known to us through the Scriptures, and of course, only a small proportion of the global earth's population started their life with a copy of The Holy Bible opened in their house. It caused me to wonder whether little children in countries such as China or India would also have been familiar with the names Adam and Eve or king Solomon. Each and every new life must begin as a blank page, and at some age and stage each of us will ask questions about our very origin and of the meaning or purpose. In some ways, I suppose that the earliest answers we receive will be a guide for each subsequent entry placed in the ever increasing book of our life.

The oldest book and therefore the oldest pages known to us in the English-speaking world is The Holy Bible. It is truly the only book that no single human being can lay claim to having compiled or own. The most that any person can claim is to be a translator of the text from its ancient pages. In this most sacred book there is found the voice and Word of God, the creator of the heavens above and global earth below. The Holy Bible continues to be the most widely circulated and read book across the globe today. Its subject is God's story of the human beings He created. It is a book of truths, mysteries and love. It provides historical facts found in no other book, instructions for living godly lives, corrections and well-intended rebukes that serve to guide every page of life into their divinely intended purpose through development, growth and unto final closure.

As a child attending church, the idea that each person's life has a distinct purpose was repeatedly taught. I have always understood that to mean events recorded on each new page of the unfolding life should reflect that godly purpose. But, of course, the purpose of a life must be discovered in order to take its full course. There can be no certainty as to just how many people even believe this to be so. How many believe that the life they are entrusted with is really not their own, but has only been gifted, for an unknown span, by the goodness of God. So believing in the very existence of God is to accept that God has set a purpose to every life. It is for each life therefore to be steered into its godly course from as early as that purpose becomes clear. From the entries on some pages of life, many persons found that godly path and purpose from an early age.

The Bible gives the history of king David, who was led into his life's purpose as a young shepherd boy by revelations given by God to the priest, Samuel. On page after page in the Old Testament books of Samuel, Kings, Chronicles and Psalms, David lived out the godly purpose for his life. His remarkable and fulfilled life would stand out as just one of many examples of how God is able to reveal His desire for the way that our lives should be lived according to His divine will and purpose. Yet neither the matter of God's will for the lives He created, nor the idea of their live was predestined with a clear purpose, are widely accepted by the vast majority of people on the globe. This is perhaps a reflection of the growing tendency in many persons to dismiss any suggestion that the life they possess and live out should be placed under the control of any source other than themselves. This is echoed in popular slogans and catchphrases of, 'It's my life, and I will do with it just what I will.'

It is estimated that some two billion persons today profess to live by the keeping and practices of the Christian tradition. This is a very significant number and of course, there are entire nations that can be identified as being "Christian countries". Some nations of Latin or South America, for example, profess full national adherence to the Christian faith promoted through the historic crusading and evangelism campaigns of the Roman Catholic Church. Thus, to be born in many of these countries today, brings a greater consciousness in the presence and supremacy of the God that is featured on the pages of the Holy Bible. That therefore gives personal reassurance that all things touching God must begin in what the Christian believer calls his or her 'faith'. That faith begins with the hearing, understanding and then belief and trust in the total and unquestioned reality of God as supreme and eternal. It is only when we trust God that we begin to obey His voice. That's what my mother was brought up to believe in her childhood home in a heavily wooded agricultural district in the eastern side of Hanover parish, on the tropical sun kissed island of Jamaica. Through a lifetime of working to survive, she learned to believe, trust and sought to obey the purpose set over her by the God of the Holy Bible. Some of the pages from the book of her life would no doubt contain many entries worthy to be erased, because they did not conform to the purpose that God may have revealed. Yet she continued to complete new pages for each day over her span of seventy-six years. As consistent with her understanding of the God in the Holy Bible, she always retained the unfailing belief that on a day in the future, even after her physical death, there would follow a final appearance before a judgement seat with God exercising due justice to reward every person according to their belief, the faith and their works. That was her belief as to the final settlement of every year destined by God for the full and complete book of the lifespan that each person was allocated.

Chapter Two
Unseen Things

As a child, my maternal grandmother, that is my mother's mum, lived in her own little house, made of timber, boards and a shiny zinc roof. There may have been twenty or so feet between one corner of our house and grandma Estry's smaller house. It was in that house that I first heard stories about ghosts and spirits. Grandma Estry attended a Baptist church in the nearest neighbouring area, two miles away. She had a soothing soft voice and loved to sing catchy little songs. She appeared to enjoy teaching me some of these. But it wasn't so much the songs that would grab and hold my attention. Rather, it was her well re-known 'duppy' or ghost stories that kept me glued near to her feet, especially as the evenings begun to darken. Those stories had the effect of making me believe there was always something evil lurking in the dark, behind every post, shadowy tree or moving leaf. Often times when she was through with a story, I would feel so scared that I refused to step out of her house. My eyes never saw a ghost but yet she had caused my mind to become convinced that something evil was outside for real. Over time, stories of spirits, demons and devils simply proliferated and passed around through several local storytellers from the oral tradition in small villages packing these into their bags for bar rooms and street corner listeners. Admittedly, not every person hearing will choose to believe the subject of many of these stories, I was captivated by these stories as a child. Grandma Estry always told her stories and would always end them with a mysterious smile all over her face.

I have come to know a thing or two about angels, spirits, demons and devil, from the Holy Bible, because God made humanity aware of these things. I have certainly learned that devils are not the only unseen sources that lurk around and about us in this world. In point of fact God is the ultimate and Supreme Spirit source, meaning to exist without any physical form, and able to exercise sovereign power and authority to control everything known in the terrestrial and material universe. The Supreme Spirit of God rules over the spirits of every other force and form.

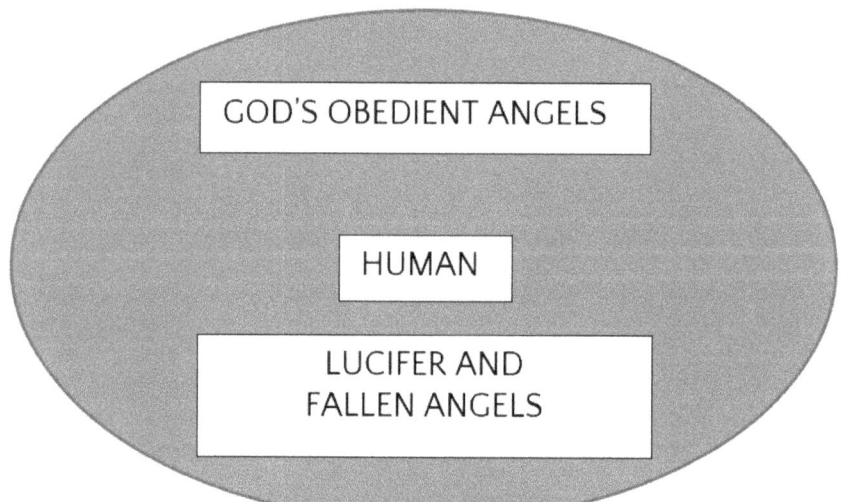

In looking at this diagram we can better understand our own position, in relation to other material, natural, physical and terrestrial things. God's creation of man, meaning humans, comprises three elements of a visible outer body, an unseen soul and an even deeper indivisible spirit. The body is of flesh, skin, bones, tissues, muscles and so forth and can be readily seen and touched. The soul includes mind, intellect, emotions, and a free will. The spirit imbeds a conscience, the deepest and most mysterious part of our being and is unique to humanity. It is through the conscience in our spirit that God will communicate. The character of God is Spirit, invisible to the naked eyes, wholesome, loving, infinite and utterly awesome. That is the God described on the pages of the Holy Bible my mother and grandmother read me as a child. I had always accepted the existence of just one eternal, infinite being, who by some supreme mystery, embraced simultaneously a union of three distinct personalities as eternal heavenly Father, eternal begotten Son, and the eternal blessed Holy Ghost. This is the Trinity of the eternal unity and oneness of God.

It was from the pages of the same Holy Bible that bad counter spirits of demons, ghosts and devils became revealed to humanity, by God. The Creator and Ruler over all things, revealed through His Word that the origin of all ungodly spirits came from one described originally as Lucifer, an angel created by God's own power. The character of Lucifer had become corrupted when his will shifted towards self-serving, covetousness, envy, jealousy and pride. So this angel of later darkness was not created corrupt. The Word of God helps us to understand that scores of angelic beings were present with God in heaven before human creation. God's Word to the prophets Isaiah and Ezekiel, would later reveal that Lucifer was a leader amongst angelic beings in heaven. But that exalted position was lost to him forever when he became puffed up in pride with his beauty and gifts, leading to coveting the most supreme exalted position of his own maker, God Almighty. The eternally uncompromising God exercised judgement and justice against Lucifer by removing him from the immediate presence around the heavenly throne. He was cast out from the presence of God to wait until the time appointed for a final eternal condemnation. The spirit of Lucifer will not die but will suffer eternal punishment, while a new heaven and earth will be established by God as reward for those living in obedience and righteousness on this present earth.

If God did not reveal in the Scriptures that it was one bad apple that would eventually spoil the character of His creation, then we could not have known about this extraordinary spirit of temptation and deception which occupies and shares the space around us. Devils have been revealed to assume many forms, including their ability to possess and occupy the flesh and mind of both humans and animals. Remembering that this source is always the errant spirit that is in Lucifer, and who was not created as flesh as we were but as an angelic spirit. Lucifer was created by God and must therefore occupy a position beneath or below God. Endowed with more extraordinary wisdom, knowledge, understanding, strength and speed than humans, Lucifer used his gift of free will to covet the highest position of his very maker and creator. So we understand angelic spirits to be higher than humans, but lower than God, the Father, Son and Holy Spirit. The natural eyes of a man cannot normally see or recognize them because they are not physical in being, form or character. We cannot see them moving amongst us. But through the eyes of Jesus Christ, the Spirit of God, Scriptures have made their presence and character fully known. Through God's revelation in the Person and Work of Jesus Christ, we have come to know that Lucifer and other angels actually existed before human creation. We have not been told just when in eternity they first came into existence, but only that all created beings are loved by God and this great truth will never change. The divine and holy character of the Supreme Almighty can never change. So we have been made to understand that in his created existence Lucifer began in the full love and reverence of the creator. There was a time past when Lucifer gave loyal worship to God. He was described as a 'chief musician' in the company of angels assembled around the heavenly throne of God. We cannot fathom the passing period of time or age of creation in eternity past but we can understand that a mutual love and harmony prevailed for some passing time, between the Creator and the created, with each in their ordained position and place. In time, it may well be that God later introduced the conscious experience of angelic liberty, freedom, choice and free will in these created beings. Maybe the windows of their spirit were made to open for the experience of God's test of obedience and righteousness. We cannot know the divine intention of the Almighty God. But He has made us understand that the angels were also granted a choice to understand and exercise free will. One aspect of knowing and fearing God springs from the revelation of His love and complete power, knowledge and infinite wisdom. After all, the angelic hosts were given the free gift of love, joy and perfect peace in God's presence. These spirit beings had responded to God at their inception with loving worship, devotion, obedience, loyalty and faithfulness. That is, until Lucifer succumbed to lust, self-desire and pride. He would exercise his free will to please himself. It was from this point that the Scriptures revealed that Lucifer corrupted one third of the angelic host in heaven, leading them to doubt the perfect love and divine motive of their creator. Two-thirds of the angelic hosts however did not fall into the eternal error under Lucifer's deception but continued in free will to worship and honour God around His heavenly throne. Thence, for Lucifer and the errant band of fallen angels in heaven, their walk into disobedience and disloyalty brought the first recordings of God's justice in judgement. They could no longer remain or prevail in the immediate presence of God and so according to the Scriptures, they were cast out from their former elevated position and place in the highest heaven.

God is the ultimate oracle of all His works. He gave the Scriptures so we will come to know Him. A knowledge of God points to His awesomeness, and causes our hearts to love and also to fear Him in righteousness. He stands high above all things, existing outside of time and nature, yet He watches all the acts of His creatures beneath. In speaking through the Scriptures God aimed to inform and instruct; correct and chastise; to train and lead us into the path of a right relationship as a perfect Father to all. We learn from the Scriptures that there is no event or occurrence from eternity past to eternity future which is not known to God. In fact, by the infinite knowledge of God, Lucifer's rebellion and his permitted presence amongst us must have been according to God's perfect plan and will.

We must understand that all things are under the controlling hands of the Almighty, whether they appear to us to be good or they are evil. It is only God that knows and can reveal His eternal plan for His creation and He alone controls His own divine will. So the choices made in free will by Lucifer and in all his other manifestations as Satan, Devil or spirits of evil, would have been foreknown to God and therefore cannot change the plan of the creator. We understand the cause for the ejection or casting out of Lucifer and the one third of disobedient and disloyal fallen angelic spirits. The Scriptures teaches that they were subjected to the righteous uncompromised judgement of their creator unto eternal condemnation. And while, by the divine will and wisdom of God, some of the errant spirits were not immediately ensnared but permitted to go through and fro in the earth, others were restricted and bound up in the darkness of hell. That is somewhere beneath the earth, where they await the time appointed by God for their final doom in a lake of eternal fire. So from our understanding of hell, that is a place of eternal doom, established by God, to detain errand and rebellious created beings, who have been removed from fellowship with God. They were created by God and received His gracious gifts of love and fullness of joy. Yet they could always accept God's truth or reject it. They had the choice offered between two destinies and one third of the number in heaven chose freely to doubt the love of God, and chose instead, to believe the vain promises of the self-serving Lucifer. They would be judged and gathered together in that place described as hell, and from where they will be joined later by their leader, Lucifer. Although hell was not made nor intended to claim human souls, it will be the final destination for both angels and human beings who rebel against God. The eternal destiny for all who doubt God's love, words and promises, without repentance or contriteness of spirit, will share the very same lake of fire.

But even so, we must also understand that it is in the divine plan of God to stir and use the satanic and devilish spirits of Lucifer for His ultimate gain. Although condemned, God in His flawless wisdom, has allowed the spirit of Lucifer to remain loose, yet within restricted limits, and retaining some of his original knowledge, powers and strength. He retains a full memory of the creator and of all spiritual things, past and present, in heaven. So although he is always under God's controlling hands, these satanic spirits have been assigned roles in God's plan until the time appointed to bring all into a final judgement, confinement and torment into eternity. But until that time of

God's appointment, human have been gifted the global earth for a temporary inhabitation. So much has been learned about God and about ourselves even from the knowledge revealed in the Scriptures, around the existence and position of angels. We were created in the love of God just as angels were created by God, in love, before us. Angels had existed for some time in a relationship of mutual love with God just as Adam and Eve, the first humans of history. But thereafter, in the attacks and tests of temptation, the spirit of Lucifer caused the human free will to be influenced, with doubts and hostility against the Creator. But God in His eternal grace did not immediately judge us in our rebellion. He has allowed us time and space to recognise the errors of walking in the spirit of Lucifer. The Holy Spirit has been given to help those who seek Him to overcome and be saved from the eternal lake of hell after the final judgement by Jesus Christ, the first fruit in the vineyard of God.

Chapter Three
First Test of Human Free Will

The natural tendencies of our flesh have always been resistant to the counsel of God's Holy Spirit. A man who is under the rule of his flesh will always move to the side of temporary pleasures, lust and pride while the Spirit of God always wants to move us to the side of permanent joy and humility. Consider Adam, a name known perhaps to every culture of the world, as the first human being that stood upon the surface of planet earth, according to God's revelation in the Scriptures. Adam was unique. His many distinctions include that of being formed or created from dust of the earth. Hence, he did not experience human conception, foetal development and no subsequent human physical birth. God equipped him with faculties of physical maturity, upon his entry into creation, the beginning of human history. We learnt that there was no other human presence at that time, so the first thing that Adam would have seen and experienced would be the presence of God, in whatever form God chose to reveal Himself. He did not therefore experience the comforting arms of a mother, or the warm intake of milk from the breast. He rested on his first day and fellowship with is creator. In life, our first conscious experiences will usually include having the presence of a mother and with whom we experience a sense of dependence, comfort, protection and trust. Another early experience is the special bond of love that we build up day by day during those most dependent phases of life. We grow and develop with further senses of position and place that we occupy under the rule of parents. Parents hold the legal right and the responsibility for moral rule over their children during their dependent years, whether they like it or not. As children we will also come to accept our own position as being subservient to any older sibling, brothers or sisters, because they arrived first in the order of birth.

In the continuing process of development, we will come to crawl on our belly, walk on unstable legs, stumble, fall and we also learn to stand up again. We learn so much about ourselves and others who are around us by these first human experiences. So Adam learnt to stand and walk by the parenting of God. Hence, he came to understand things his eyes could see, such as the body, its members and their position, function and so on. He would have been the first to receive

God's gracious gifts of wisdom, knowledge and understanding, among others. So when he stumbled or fell down, he learnt to stand up again by understanding the desires of God for him to walk upright. By the sense of his eyes Adam would have known his own body of flesh. He would come to know that God is not Himself of flesh and blood. So although he was in the presence of God, he would not have seen God in the form of human flesh. He would likely only experience the presence through the inward working of God's Spirit. Because God is Spirit, not flesh. Yet, unlike the angels who were created and given life before him as spirit beings, Adam came into physical life as flesh and bones, with a moral likeness in the sense of being made aware of things that would please or displease his creator. Adam's body of flesh was designed for inhabiting the atmosphere of planetary earth, and not the spiritual space of heaven above where angelic beings exist with God. Adam was sustained by God in every way. But that condition would depend upon Adam's future conduct, meaning that by his own free will he could either live in full trust, dependence and obedience or rebel and depart from the presence of his creator. He would later rebel against the moral boundary set for him by God and thereafter faced a penalty of physical and spiritual death. In physical death, the mass of flesh gathered from the dust of the earth would decay and be returned to the very earth from where it had been gathered.

Over time, I have tended to think of this story of the first created human as God's starting lesson for us about both Himself and about us. It is as though God was presenting an object warning to us, through Adam. I believe that God was teaching us about His sovereign right and power over all created things. On the same sixth day of Adam's creation, God also made all other living beasts, animals and other physical life forms. Later, when all creatures were brought before Adam he would have seen that all of them walked in obedience to God. This was also where Adam would get a first test on whether he understood the difference between himself and the other life forms. He was allowed to give names to the animals and this was perhaps a way of giving Adam a sense of dominion over them. But he had also to show that he understood the difference between himself as human, made with a spirit and conscience and, the animals, having no spirit or conscience. Adam did not choose any of the animals as a suited companion because he realised that he was human and not a beast or animal. God had made him aware of the difference in standards of behaviour, conduct and responsibility. In the role as Father, God first protected, counselled and then released humans unto the rule of an inner conscience to determine and exercise choices. God had demonstrated to Adam that He was a loving, caring, compassionate and all sufficient parent.

There are at least three other important lessons that I can grasp from the way that God chose to make Himself known to us through the creation and history of Adam. Firstly, there is no beginning with God because He exists eternally, meaning that He is always and forever. Every human being can be destroyed; every flesh will perish one day. But this is not so with God. He revealed Himself to mark the beginning point of human existence, not His own, and He will be present at the end point of human existence, and into eternity. Secondly, our eyes will not see God in the way that we can see a human parent because He is a Spirit. Within every human being God has deposited within us some portion of that same spirit or likeness. This makes us aware of His presence, though invisible to our natural eyes. By His Omni-present or ever present character, we can sense that God is present everywhere and all the times. Thirdly, the character of God is also Omni-potent, meaning that He possesses all force and power. So powerful is God that His very Word can be likened in effect to a two-edged sword, meaning that nothing can stand in the way of them accomplishing their intent and purpose. It is of the truth that the best master builder cannot speak a physical structure into existence, yet God speaks and the effect of His Word brings into being land and sea, darkness and light.

That lesson was therefore, about how to recognise the love and fullness of joy in the presence of God. That fullness would become an experience of spiritual emptiness when Adam transgressed sometime after his creation. Today, everyone who hear, or read and understand the object lesson from the Genesis narrative of Adam's creation and fall, must accept that the devilish spirits of lust and pride in the natural flesh played their part in separating humans from the eternal Spirit of God. Yet in His love and mercy, a way was left for the spirit in each and every human to become reconnected to the Creator.

Chapter Four
A Tropical Childhood

I am a product of a deep rural tropical childhood. But instead of saying rural, many people will just say, 'country living', and this conjures up images of the natural environment, sparse population, wild and green forestry, bad weeds, overgrown shrubs, grass valleys with a mix of vegetation and agricultural provisions. Rural living have all of these features plus many more. My earliest years were probably as gratifying as it could get for me. It was the friendliest place and time that I experienced. It may have been as safe and secure a time as it could be and, as for exposure to nature, the cycle of sunshine and rainfall with every seasonal fruit, could be taken as signs of special blessings falling all over the land. Our area has been called a district, meaning adjoined to other larger areas and in order to receive local government or municipal services and facilities such as primary and secondary education. It meant that at the age of five or six years, children from our area would be registered to attend the nearest primary school in another area. Our district sat on high mountainous slopes, high above the level of the sea coast and which pass through the neighbouring area of Sandy Bay, a traditional fishing town. So children walked down the hill to attend school. It was in the school environment that I recall the first bad taste of rivalry. It was in fact the case that to have come from a deeper rural community brought the unflattering label of living at the 'back', as opposed to the front, which was given to areas located nearer to the coastal plains surrounding the beautiful Caribbean Sea or a busy passing main road.

The history of my own family in the area has been traced back to the years following slave emancipation. The patriarch of our family was believed to have travelled from the cane fields of Hamden, in Trelawny parish, moving westward through banana and sugar cane growing fields in Somerton, near Montego Bay, before settling on the hills near the Maggoty plantation on the eastern side of Hanover. In those early days of freedom and the liberty to move, labouring men poured out their physical strength into securing and working up small plots of ground for provisions such as yam, banana, and vegetable gardens, consuming part and also selling on any excess. For many children growing up in deep, deeper or deepest rural families a hundred plus years later, in the 1970s, their daily normal would include living in close proximity with various domestic animals such as goats, pigs and cows. But it could also mean living long distances from main passing roads, public health facilities, schools, transportation, electricity, running water, policing, courts and security services. Rural inhabitants would very often be spoken of by not so rural dwellers as being 'country people', and this took on more derogatory and insulting undertones for "backwardness", "uncivilised', 'behind time', 'back-a-bush', colloquially, and 'behind the world'. The children in Sandy Bay saw themselves as belonging to a 'town', and I guess that they would develop a different mind-set, regarding themselves and their area to be better. So it became a custom that we would always be greeted with much derision by those not-so-rural children of our closest neighbouring area. For one thing, many children from our community didn't sport any sort of footwear on a daily basis, but often walked down the hill bare footed. Some may have been fortunate enough to own just one pair of shoes in those days and this would be worn only to school and church. This may not have been the way or style for our neighbours on the sea coastal bay area. They would wear some form of footwear, such as rubber slippers or loafers. Fact is that there was no main sun baked asphalt road in our area. We walked mainly on grass verges and foot tracks to attend basic school or church. Some of these tracks would become widened by the tyre tracks of the few vehicles present or visiting the area at that time.

Another feature of our deep rural district community life of the 1970s was that electrical light circuits had not yet been fully introduced, and when it arrived at first, there could only be access by those houses located nearest to our single stone pebbled road. But this was not the experience of our neighbours on the front in Sandy Bay. So our neighbours would gleefully remind us that they were living in the light of human civilization while we were 'dark bush people'. Some of the less bold children from our community would hear these words of torment daily and the barrage of mockery and insults became off putting for many. Yet another subject of derision levelled against us was a failure by many going down the hill to come to grips with basic reading and writing. This endured as a bad scourge against children from our community and made many feel even lower in their self-esteem. In many cases the persistent provocation and daily taunts drew acts of physical retaliation. This at times led into a circle of playground fights and falling under the heavy whip-hand of school teachers who could freely administer corporal punishment at that time. Many of the tougher children from our district would take up matters into their own hands in the daily school yard banter.

I probably became aware of the sense of injustice during those early primary years at the school in Sandy Bay. Whether on the walk back up the hill to home or down for school each day there would be tales shared about the injustice meted out against children from our area by the teachers. The sense of injustice could take on the form of who was judged to be right or wrong when a conflict or fight broke out between children from our two areas. I can still remember that there was a special room set aside in the school for unruly children called 'the jail'. It was used to detain mainly older and tougher boys who got appended by the teachers during a school yard fight. The detained would be placed in the school jail and the door locked while teaching sessions were still taking place. It would be at the end of the school day that one or more of the stronger male teachers would exercise judgement and administer beatings on the guilty party. The boy given wrong would be lashed with the school principal's cane or strap. This was a matter of deep grievance for children from our area as the accusation would invariably be that the scale of justice was never balanced. Over generations and for many years the same complaints against school yard injustice would continue, and reach the point of zero faith in school justice. In defending their lion's share of favours in school yard judgement when disagreement or fights broke out the rival Sandy Bay children would hurl taunts and insults at our generally low reading and writing abilities.

Running comments heard from many of the teachers would often lean towards the conclusion that a lack of literacy skills was cause for disruptive behaviour. This is an association that would endure beyond our school days.

There is always a direct link between functional literacy, meaning to be able to read and write the basics of your own name and address, went with disruptive behaviour. Common sense will say that the more children at a school who develop basic skills of reading and writing then the more conducive the learning environment and disciplined such a school will be. This also links into the wider global ideal for developing a literate people in a civilised culture in much the same way as England and America, among other more advanced nations. Any serious deficit will always be to the detriment of any nation, and especially such small enclaves of deepest, deeper and deep rural communities in small nations such as Jamaica. The concern about functional literacy did not end when the children from our community completed their compulsory school attending years. But it would continue into a lifetime as members of our small community churches. There is perhaps a source of deep irony in that every church adopts the feature of hosting a teaching ministry such as Sabbath or Sunday school. The Bible is the one book that is turned open every time the door of a church opens. We can also add the fact that a copy of the Bible will likely be found in almost every home in our community, when perhaps no other book will be present.

The very logical view is that there has long remained this weakness in functional reading and writing skills amongst the membership of our small rural communities, and by extension, churches. This ought not to have been hidden or treated as secret in any congregation that wants to foster meaningful participation in worship and weekly fellowship. There will ever be a need for members to share in the reading of the Word of God. After all, it is the same God whom many entered through the doors of the building to worship who also revealed Himself through His written Word, so we should therefore encourage one another to seek after His voice on the page. Most professed believers would accept that the primary purpose of our church is to guide us into a proper understanding of the righteousness and justice that will be approved by God. The Christian faith declares full acceptance of God's free offer of salvation through the life and works of Jesus Christ. This is the only way for the believer, the only truth and the only life that leads back to God, the creator. Hence, there is an immeasurable benefit to all those who will hear the Word of God, but of equal importance, understand what they hear and be encouraged to do further reading and searching of the Scriptures. While we can accept that not every believer will hear and understand at the same rate or in the same fashion, it is under the power of God, the

Holy Spirit, that all learning in church must take place. The Spirit of God moves and works to overcome disadvantages for the glory of God. We cannot doubt that God can make the slow reader pick up great speed in recognizing letters and understanding words. But that learner must first be guided by the right attitude for learning in order to gain this benefit from the enabling work of the Spirit of God. Facts be told, none of us can ever take it all in completely. A faithful believer especially needs the spiritual food of the Word as breadth out by God. The ability to take some things in by reading, even a little portion each day, will prove most helpful to the development of our ability to understand God.

CHAPTER FIVE
A Place of Worship

My paternal grandfather, that is my father's daddy, Samuel Riggan, was born in Mount Pelier district, on the second day of March, 1886. This just happened to be the very same year in which the trademark 'Church of God' name made its entry onto the landscape of religious organisations registered in the United States of America. This was an offshoot from what became known as the 'Pentecostal Holiness Movement'. These were believers seeking to follow the teachings of Jesus Christ and stand holy, sanctified and perfect with God. Disagreement in the interpretation of God's Word would cause divisions among the leading theological minds amongst that Movement and from there at least two of the earliest Pentecostal groups would emerge, namely the Holiness Church and the Church of God, respectively. Some years later, the Church of God would itself suffer a further division, and from this an additional name, the

Church of God of Prophecy, would emerge, in the years before 1953. The devil is the original liar and he could not derail the mission of the Church of God. In the difficult years falling between 1900 and 1945, with the globe seeing two devastating world wars, a health pandemic brought by the Spanish Flu, followed by a deep economic depression, missionary work by the Church of God would increase bountifully. It was during this period that the expansion of many denominations reached Jamaica and the wider Caribbean region.

Apparently, when the first attempts were made by the Church at Cleveland in Tennessee to legally register their name in Jamaica, several legal and technical challenges surfaced. It would become known that some other unconnected denomination had already registered the same 'Church of God' name as a religious organisation on the island! God would prove the devil a liar again and the church at Cleveland, Tennessee, resorted to use and register the alternative name of 'New Testament Church of God,' under its umbrella instead. Public records indicate that several well established British Christian denominations and their churches were already present in Jamaica during that same period and were actively evangelizing communities in cities, towns and in rural villages. These included the Ireland imported Roman Catholics, English Anglicans, Scottish Presbyterians, Welsh Methodists and Baptists. The Church of God, rooted in Cleveland, Tennessee, would become an addition to that pool and brought with them a new Pentecostalism. The island capital City of Kingston was their first point of entry, apparently through contacts initiated by a local preacher, identified as Reverend J. Wilson Bell, in the midst of the First World War, 1917. It was from there that public exhortations on the finished work of Jesus Christ for our salvation began to win souls for the kingdom of heaven, under the banner of the Church of God, Cleveland, Tennessee. The Word of the Gospel of Jesus Christ would continue to go forth, from 'preaching stations' established in areas of Kingston, before reaching neighbouring St. Catherine and Clarendon after a few years.

The name of Jesus Christ brings victory, and under this new legal identity in Jamaica, the denomination flourished, with the first recognized 'New Testament Church of God' emerging firmly at Mount Providence, Clarendon, around 1925. That was followed by the planting of churches in neighbouring areas at Borobridge, Frankfield, Blackwoods and Anien Town in the same parish. The move of God's Holy Spirit is never predictable and by the year 1937, the mighty Pentecostal wind would move at least one witness to the introduction of the New Testament Church of God in northern Clarendon to the western side of the island. It was in Hanover, in the deep rural community of Jericho/Claremont that one diligent servant of the Lord would arrive to begin the further spreading of the Good News Gospel of Jesus Christ. His hard labour, sometimes amidst many physical persecutions and legal trials, gave birth to the very first New Testament Church of God on the western side of the island of Jamaica, in 1937. The name of 'Brother Bailey,' the tireless evangelist of the Gospel of Jesus Christ, would become etched in the annals of this faithful and historic church at Claremont district, Hanover.

There would be more triumphs ahead for the Church of God, at Cleveland, Tennessee, and for the New Testament Church of God, as its expansion across Hanover eastern reached the community of Mount Pelier, in the year 1953. My father was also born in Mount Pelier, on the fourth day of August, 1921. He would later meet my mother in the neighbouring district of Cascade, where he lived and worked at the time. They got married and later came to live in Mount Pelier in October, that same year. My mother would actually be in the founding group of members and therefore witnessed the introduction of the New Testament Church of God into the community.

At around the time of my childhood the population of the district numbered around two hundred and fifty households and was well served by five different denominations and churches. But only three of these had a building for meetings in the local area. In its own way, each would contribute to our understanding of the Christian faith, Pentecostal worship and of the Triune God, the Eternal Father of all creation, the Son and Saviour, Jesus Christ and the empowering Holy Spirit.

The oldest denomination to arrive in the area may well have been the 'Street Band' or 'Pukkumania Revivalist Zion Church'. Wide following for this church had existed in small meeting groups among slaves for more than three hundred years. They adopted a flexible structure in organisation and worship with a unique mode of African rituals, mixed with forms of Western Christian beliefs and religious practices. They would expand around the island after the 1834 slave emancipation, with members dressing in similar bright coloured bandana clothing and head wraps. They would march through areas, with heavy drum beating and African ancestral dancing. Heavy foot stomping and gestures of smiting hands may well speak to traditions connected with the religious rituals of West African slaves who were kidnapped and transported to Jamaica from their motherland. The people in many rural communities such as in Mount Pelier would have been drawn by the marching and to the rhythm of their drumming. Various myths, legends and superstitions of the capture and release of 'Ancestral Spirits', followed those associated with Pukkumania and as a child I developed a consciousness of ghosts and the idea of there being evil workings of obeah or 'Black Magic', in the community. The marches continued to pass through the district for many years before a female leader, referred to as a 'Mother Woman', emerged around 1951. Her home would become the 'Band's Yard', and base for their Sunday and Wednesday evening meetings. The Pukkumania Revivalist Zion Church subscribed to a different mix of cultural traditions and religious practices and they would no doubt become the primary target of rebukes and rebuttals for the later arriving Baptist and more spirited New Testament Pentecostal branded churches.

The Baptist Union had members and followers in the community and possessed a strong history on the island that dates back to the time of slavery. In fact, three of the island's national heroes, Paul Bogle, George William Gordon and Samuel Sharpe may have been active Baptist Union church leaders, before each in their own turn went to the gallows because they supported the call to abolish forced African slave trading and transportation up to 1834. Historically, Baptist missionaries had a long presence on the island and they would always move quickly into areas with freed Africans. In the parish of Hanover, the growing population clustering close to former slave plantations at Tryall and Maggoty would have drawn their attention. The lush green landmass which Mount Pelier occupied can be seen climbing up slopes and sliding onto flat grassy plains close to long established commercial banana exporting plantations, sugar cane fields, cattle pens and coconut orchards, between Cascade to the west and Tryall to the east. The earliest occupants settled around the late-1800s with travelling labourers coming to the Maggoty cash cropping farms and sugar cane estates. The high green hills attracted independent minded animal breeders, cow herders, trench cutters and ground farmers and a steady increase in its residents continued throughout the 1900s up to 1960s. The Baptist church was seen as a defender of the free local communities and the names of many of their leaders would no doubt draw followers into their churches. I have never been certain as to whether a separate European brand of the Baptist church actually exists apart and independent of the American Southern Baptists that we associate today with the protests of Dr Martin Luther King during the 1950s and 60s. But that charismatic styled Baptist church leadership was not seen in Mount Pelier, where it cuts a much quieter and reserved presence at meetings and worship. They did not make a public display of the 'fire and judgement', brand of charismatic Pentecostal preaching, Holy Spirit baptism, speaking in tongues or made professions of divine healing as characterised the New Testament Church of God. My maternal grandmother, Estry, became a member of the Baptist church, from its base in Sandy Bay, and she simply joined with others to walk two miles downhill and then walk up again every Sunday morning. It would not be until the early 1990s that a local building for the Baptist church would materialise.

It may be accurate to state that all the other churches that became established in the community after the 1940s emerged from the labour of American evangelical Pentecostal Christian missionaries and local evangelists. The New Testament Church of God arrived in the area, 1953, and would have sought to set fire, as it were, to the mixed worship and African cultural rituals of the Pukkumania especially. I am quite certain that they would have made every godly effort to redirect local people away from membership and bands yard meetings. The beliefs and values of these two churches would no doubt collide in competition for new converts willing to seek after the way to eternal life and salvation.

So by all accounts the district had been well served by Christian missionaries and evangelized for over seven decades to date. The ultimate purpose of any church, established in the name of God, must be to spread the gospel message that God sent to us by the mouth of His only begotten Son, Jesus. This is the 'Good News' message of the free gift of salvation which God has made available to all who will believe in the name, Person and atoning work of His Anointed Son, Jesus the Christ. It is to this eternal end that the long list of pastors and evangelists who climbed up to the top of the hill into Mount Pelier district, came to proclaim. In their turn, ministers have preached up some mighty storms and sent out dire warnings about God's promised judgement of brimstone and fire, the ultimate penalty for living in sin. As a child I heard many sermons with such dire overtones and dramatic contents and I also listened to the testimony of many people who have accepted water baptism after the great efforts by prophets, pastors and evangelists. We learn from Scriptures that the Word of God was given through the power of the Holy Spirit and which brings about conviction and transformation, starting with the heart and innermost parts. Yet for some reason, successive generations in the district have remained largely unchanged in the outward expression of their words and deeds. In spite of the many churches and their frequent meetings, evangelism and missions, precious few among professed believers have displayed any fruit from their claims of Holy Spirit filled testimonies. Many professed Christians have continued to struggle daily to quell the stronghold of natural lusts of the flesh and eyes.

The New Testament church at Mount Pelier was established after the likes of Claremont, Lucea and Cascade, among others, in areas of Hanover eastern. The church at Cascade was the first 'District Church' to oversee or supervise Mount Pelier but that position changed after Sandy Bay was planted and established some years later and installed as a district church. But it is certainly the case that the Mount Pelier church was established first of the two. On the whole, district churches tend to be larger in congregations or membership. There was always a credentialed Bishop appointed to lead them rather than the lower ranked exhorter or pastors. It was usually the case during my childhood years that when a local church scheduled a week-long calendar of evangelistic revival meetings, for example, the district church would play a leading role to organise the services, since such events would be expected to receive interests and attendance from neighbouring areas also.

We continued to be a New Testament Church attending family and for those in the community who did not attend a church during my childhood years the voices of many Pentecostal preachers would still reach into their homes. My mother was an avid radio listener in her time and we always possessed a small battery powered transistor radio at our house. It would be turned on every morning at around six o'clock for the early morning news and would continue to play through most of the morning. Then it would be turned off again to save the batteries before being turned on again around the time of the daily mid-day and six o'clock for evening news. We did not own any television sets at that time, so the radio was the means of hearing news and public information daily. My mother listened to both local stations and the English speaking British Broadcasting Corporation (BBC) World Service for international news. But she especially looked forward to the broadcasting of church meetings and those hosted by the well-known American Evangelist, Billy Graham. His broadcast days may have been on either Saturday or Sunday, I don't remember which for certain. I can recall that he was preaching on the radio on days when I was not at school. The Reverend Billy Graham, as he was titled, was very charismatic in his radio voice and persona. I believe he preached the Christian Gospel of Jesus Christ with great clarity. My mother loved to listen to him and did not miss many of these radio broadcasts. But closer to home, she would also listen to radio broadcasts by local preachers such as the brothers Ronald, Wellesley or Herro Blair. My mother said that the Blair family had originated from another parish, 'up the line', meaning eastward from Hanover, in neighbouring St. James. The father was Pastor Mortimer Blair, and he became a Pentecostal preacher. He was the first pastor appointed to lead the church at Mount Pelier when it became established in 1953. He was as father of four prominent preaching sons, with two of these, Ronald and Wellesley, serving the New Testament Church of God in Jamaica as former Island Overseers. 'Daddy Blair' would have laboured very hard in our area during those difficult and uncertain days. He would have taken up the charge to wrestle in Mount Pelier with rival factions from the Church of God of Prophecy, as well as the Pukkumania Revivalist Zion Church. Daddy Blair would have served in the strength and enabling of the Holy Spirit of God and he clearly won those battles, going on to establish the early foundation of the New Testament Church of God at Mount Pelier.

CHAPTER SIX
GATHER*ing The Church*

It is common for us to simply refer to the building in which people meet for collective or corporate worship as, 'the Church.' There are lots of words that could be used generally to describe the coming together of people. Meetings can take place in many different settings and for various purposes. Take for example, a Parliament, where politicians will meet together. But we would not refer to politicians as keeping church. It is for the purpose of the meeting that will define a gathering by many people in one place at the same time. It was the ancient Greeks who first offered a word, *'ekklisia' in the Scriptures,* to mean a gathering for the purpose of worship. When Bible translators introduced it into English the meaning behind the word was of people who shared a belief by faith in the risen Jesus Christ, being brought together by God's Holy Spirit, in service and worship. So the word, 'church', in English, was not originally used or intended to be a description of just any gathering or building.

The first New Testament reference to the word, 'church' came from Jesus ahead of His going to the cross at Calvary, in full obedience to God's will. The understanding of what Jesus meant when speaking to His disciples about 'the rock' on which He would 'build His church', became clear only after His death, resurrection and ascension back into the presence of God the Father in heaven. There was a clear understanding of the word church, and its meaning implied only true believers, convicted by faith, who would walk and live in oneness as the spiritual representation of Jesus Christ on earth. So only true believers who abide in obedience and fellowship with Christ would comprise the church according to the New Testament Bible.

Today we have arrived at such a deepening and deafening confusion about just who or what should be called a church. Yet there was no confusion in Jesus when He made known the will of God to move humanity into a New Testament age, and guided by the presence and work of the Holy Spirit to call out His church from the world. No reference was made to the church in the Old Testament Scriptures. This was a deep mystery kept hidden from all previous ages and generations. At that point in time when God sent His Son, Jesus, into the world as Saviour from the bondage of Satan, the age of the Old

Testament came to a close, with the rule of Moses laws, wars between nations and condemnation to death and hell. A new age would begin when Jesus Christ conquered Satan, death, and the grave and ascended back to the right hand of the Father in heaven. The Person of the Holy Spirit was then sent to dwell with humanity permanently, to comfort, counsel and guide unto godliness and will be available until such time as the Father determines to rapture or call home from the earth those who will be rewarded for overcoming sin and the world.

Today we reference our understanding of the church with the body of Christ, gathered and transformed by the Holy Spirit, to continue the Christian mission that is to lead repentant and redeemed humanity back to God. But that body of Christ, must remain united on this earth, doing good works and providing a beacon of light to a spiritually dark globe. While Jesus walked the dry and dusty land of ancient Palestine two thousand years ago, He represented the will of God the Father. He was equally God in all His attributes and character but was cast in incarnate human flesh, as the person of God the Son. The shining glory of the Son could only be revealed by the Father. So, this was part of what God revealed to Peter when Jesus put the question recorded in St. Matthew, chapter 16:15, to the disciples: 'But whom say ye that I am?' It was Peter who received a divine burst of revelation from God and declared Jesus's true identity, when he answered, saying, "Thou art the Christ, the Son of the living God.' In verse 17, Jesus affirmed God's revelation to Peter, when He said, 'For flesh and blood hath not revealed it unto thee, but My Father which is in heaven.' It was this revelation of the divine essence of Jesus as God in the flesh that led up to that first mention of the word which became translated as 'church' in all the New Testament Scriptures. Jesus then revealed the further mystery of God's will to establish the impending church on the strength of this sacred truth when He further declared to Peter, in the same passage from St. Matthew, 'and upon this rock I will build my church; and the gates of hell shall not prevail against it.'

Further down in the order of the New Testament Scriptures the book of Acts provided us with a history of how that revealed church would become established. All the things of God must be set forth and be accomplished and the church became a reality on the Day of Pentecost more than two thousand years ago. So that revelation of the church and what it would be, could not therefore be understood to mean any building of wood or blocks. At best the understanding should be of an earthly presence of the spiritual reality that is Christ. This is therefore my understanding of the word as translated from the Greek 'ekklesia', to the English, 'church.' So, the Holy Spirit had the charge to follow after Jesus, to do the work of gathering and transforming fickle earthly flesh for the spiritual body of Christ. He will select and transform those who are faithful and true to the commands and instructions of Jesus Christ. He possesses all the attributes of God and so can see into the heart of every professed Christian believer. He will do the work to gather according to the righteous and holy standard of God the Father.

From ever since the sending of the Holy Spirit fully into the world for this specific purpose of gathering souls for the body of Christ, many men have laid presumptuous claims to be included in that body. But God has not made public the names or number or physical identity of the true believers gathered by the Holy Spirit. This will only be revealed on that day of our final judgement, according to the certain promises of God, when Jesus Christ will stand upon the surface of this earth a second time, the Second Advent. He will not be covered in perishable flesh on that occasion, but will stand in all power and heavenly glory. So while many buildings carry the written label of being a 'church', in all truth, there can be no meaningful church of any name, established on this earth, unless it is gathered by the power of the Holy Spirit. All work by the Holy Spirit is done unto God. This work will receive full and final approval by Jesus Christ, who now possesses all authority and power from God the Father. So there can be no building or assembly acceptable unto God that is coming from just the hands and choices of men. In the absence of God's Holy Spirit such an instrument will be under the power of Satan's benign and evil imitating spirits. Because the Scriptures revealed that while God has sent one Holy Spirit into the world, the active and evil workings of Satan and his many rebellious angelic beings have released many false and counterfeit spirits into the world. They are able to influence the self-driven motives and claims of many professed believers. Yet it is also made clear in Scriptures that the Spirit of God and those released by Satan and other devils will never dwell together in the same place. Therefore, where God's Holy Spirit indwells, this will be evidenced by a gifting of power and special enablement for service unto God alone. If any meeting is not under the power of God's Holy Spirit, the display of ungodliness will become apparent with deception, strife, uncleanness, malice, personal power struggles and in other likeness of Satan's character. So it has been made abundantly clear in the Scriptures that a church is not a building or in a widely published and legally registered name. It is instead a gathering by the Holy Spirit, in the will of God, as the visible earthly presence of the spiritual body of Christ. It is only present in a transitory state, but only for a time as determined by God the Father.

In the two thousand years since the revelation was made by Jesus to the apostle Peter, many men have continued to do their own independent gathering and building up of their own churches. Across the small island landscape of Jamaica, there can perhaps be found the highest concentration of 'churches', per square mile, as compared to anywhere else under the sun.

This is a quite incredible phenomenon, in and of itself. Perhaps this is made all the more incredible when given that only God's Holy Spirit has that authority to gather into the body that Jesus called 'his church.' Hence, if the founding of each and every named church on the island had truly come from a gathering work by the Holy Spirit then the people on this island should be counted to be among the most blessed. Such godly fruit which marks the outward evidence of God's Holy Spirit should be seen every day and everywhere across the full length and width of the island's geographical span. After all, the calculated ratio of population count to the number of denominations is somewhere in the order of six or seven out of every ten persons. So by this measure there should be only a small minority left outside of the gathering present in the thousands of self-proclaimed churches. But low and behold, if such gatherings have not been at the hands of the Holy Spirit, then we face a serious and dangerous reality of suffering a deep deception over the island by Satan's false and imitating spirits. The outward evidence of their destructive works will be evident in the presence and practice of idolatry, witchcraft, hatred, wrath, strife, envying, murders, revelling, and such like. This would therefore mean that the gifting of spiritual discernment is completely absent from the island and is an indication that the Spirit of God is not really at work in many man-gathered churches and meetings of the many professed 'true' believers.

Such a depraved state and hold of false spirits over any nation will bring only the reproach of God, and the condemnation for every sinful claim unto eternal death.

Chapter Seven
A Pentecostal Christian Upbringing

There are many routes and paths that could lead a person into membership of a church. But often times this path will be rooted in familiarity with a particular local church or with people that already attend. As a child, I went to the New Testament Church of God with my mother. She said this was our family church and that had been the case since before my birth and childhood. Four older siblings had already been baptised and were members of the church. In fact, my oldest brother went on to become trained and credentialed as an ordained pastor and later, bishop in this same denomination. As a child I can well recall a framed picture which was mounted onto a piece of black canvas material in our house and which bears the words: "The Family Who Prays Together Stays Together". My eyes must have crossed those words several times each day. In later years I have sometimes reflected upon those words and would later come to understand their importance. My mother believed in the power and real effect of prayers. There were times when I recall her praying out aloud in the bedroom. Often the voice was broken up by emotions pouring out from somewhere deep down in her soul. It was her mouth that taught each of her nine children to believe in God. Before going off to sleep each night, she would insist that a prayer of thanks was said to God. She liked to pray over her children and would often repeat that our prayers will make a burden lighter and a debt cleared.

From as early as I could recall, the word 'family', or some similar sounding variation, was repeated in our house in good grace. It is of a fact that our family name extends across the district. This is so much so that several other family surnames are also very closely attached to it at their root. The family name had been likely present in the area since the 1870s. It was widely repeated that some older members of the family had dedicated some of the ground at the foot of 'Riggan Hill', for raising up the first New Testament Church building, using board and zinc. One of my uncles was later appointed as a deacon in the church. Loyalty and support by the family to the church continues to this very day. My mother had come to the area from the neighbouring Cascade district, taking up residence in Mount Pelier in early 1953 when she married my father. The first ever church structure was completed around that time. I can well remember as a child the simple look inside the building. Before electricity became available, they made use of just two lanterns to illuminate the building at nighttime meetings. There was a high pulpit at the front with four or five red polished wooden steps to one side and which became the focal point of preaching in every meeting. My mother was also a very strong reader and writer, and this was perhaps quite unusual for a woman of her generation who was not from a white skinned or very light brown family in complexion. But she had somehow managed to become literate. She had been born and raised in what was then recorded as 'Brownsville district', which was later replaced by the district name of Cascade. But in any case she had attended both the Brownsville elementary school and the Methodist church on the same grounds, during her own childhood. The New Testament church at Cascade would have been established when she entered adulthood, and she likely would have been baptised there. When she arrived in Mount Pelier, she would simply transfer her membership to the New Testament Church, pastored at that time by the late and well known Mortimer Blair, and the father of perhaps the best known New Testament church family on the island. I believe that at least four of Pastor Blair's sons became highly esteemed church leaders over the following seven decades in Jamaica.

My mother served our local church as a Sunday school teacher for adults and fulfilled this role for many years. Her time in the area was interrupted when she left for England early in 1961, but she returned to the church after coming back from England four years later. So, in my turn, I had simply followed a line of five older brothers and three sisters into attendance and membership at the church. This was our family church and my mother was especially loyal in giving service and support to its ministers in her time. When my oldest brother entered pastoral ministry, this served to effectively complete a full circle of the family's close association with the church in the district. Over time only one of my sisters remained at the church from cradle to adulthood and now into her retirement years. She fulfilled the duties of clerk or treasurer for more than five decades. As a child attending the church there were many people who were still members at the church who had grown up with my siblings and were apt to tell me how much I looked or talked or behaved much like this or that older brother who attended the church before my time. Familiarity is a strong feature in small rural communities. There will always be people who are more familiar with your own family characters and history, even more so than you are, and whether these be hidden or open, good, bad or indifferent.

There are several very often quoted verses in the book of Proverbs, in the Bible, that speaks to the training up of a child in the manner that will please God. Most of these verses are believed to have been written by Solomon, the son of king David and the third king of ancient Israel. In one of his proverb,

Solomon wrote in the manner of a cultured modern-day poet, when he said, 'Train the child in the way he should go so that when he is older, he will not depart from it.' The God given wisdom from the verse has never lost its currency, and will always be relevant for caring parents to apply and is for all generations and human culture on our global planet earth. I too believe in the laying down of a good, firm and solid moral foundation in children as they grow in self-awareness and in moral consciousness. The parent who succeeds at instilling the most positive moral standards in their children will contribute immeasurably to their family, the community and their country, at the very least. Because these are always good principles to follow in life and if more people would carry them forward into each succeeding generation, then what a wonderful world this would be for all of us.

One of the great long-term benefits from my childhood attending church is the early exposure to the moral teachings from the Bible. As a child I came to understand from biblical teachings that you should not tell lies, nor steal. You are told not to be cruel to people or to animals and so forth. Most children were taught lessons about living in love and in peace and to care and be helpful to others. When these simple Christian principles are learnt early in your life and they are carried forward and applied in adulthood, the benefits can never be measured. We all know that when we steal anything, for example, this is an act of trespass against the possession of another person. The Bible teaches that to steal will displease God. Anything or any action that displeases God will be declared to be a 'sin'. In many ways the wilful acts of human trespass in the past have set forth countless present and future problems across the global world. Trespass against ancient Africa, through slavery, would yield the bad fruit of racial discrimination and hostility many centuries later. Similarly, trespass against Asians and Arabs have continued to provoke conflicts even today, while the same can be said about the trespasses against ancient American Indians. All of these ungodly trespasses have amounted to the planting of man-made seeds for future wars, strife, famines, pestilence and the likes.

There are processes by and through which a child will come to accept the principles and practices of Biblical morality and there can be no better place to begin than in Christianity, a global worldwide religion which is founded upon godly morals. A first step in this process always begins with hearing the Word of God as presented in the Bible. So as children some of us got exposed to the Word of God, in the written form, taught, spoken from pulpits, song through hymns and otherwise. One of the more important things is that the process of understanding moral standards begins in the Word of God. From having heard the Word of the Bible as a first step, a second step in the process would be that of understanding the things heard. Hence, our hearing and understanding necessarily work together in the process of learning. In the case of the Bible this would relate also to understanding such behaviour or conduct that will either please or displease. That which displeases God is a transgression (meaning to go away from a standard which God will accept). The foundational things that caused God's human creation to become separated from Him are the presence, practice and the rule of sin in our lives.

Chapter Eight
Train The Child

As a young child, I understood the term 'school' to mean a place where you would be sent to learn how to read and write. I never taught of our house as a school, even though my mother used our open veranda to teach groups of seven or eight adults in basic reading and writing on two evenings each week, in a contract with the government designed JAMAL (Jamaica Adult Learning) programme that was launched during the mid-1970s. I may have been around three years old when I first attended a basic school in our community. The owner and teacher was our cousin, named William, but better known as 'Mass Will'. His school was in addition to the one established and run by the government's Ministry of Education in the community. The other was the official government built and staffed basic school. It was always a thrill for me to begin to get dressed in short khaki trousers and a matching shirt, with my black slate and white chalk pencil for writing. It looked and felt like school because there were other children attending also and we had a set time for the ringing bell, which indicated the start of the school day. As I recall now, there was only one rectangular shaped room, perhaps fifteen feet by ten feet. We sat on small children sized wooden chairs, and held or balanced the writing slates on our knees. I don't remember there being desks or tables. Break times were before and after lunch and going home time was probably at 2: 30 PM. I always attended school for the five consecutive days, Monday morning until Friday. There were some children who were present for just one day, and some for two or three days each week. For three years this was my school. As we got older each September, there would always be a starting group and a leaving group. We were separated into age groups and this meant a change of seating position where the older children sat facing the blackboard while the younger ones faced the opposite end of the room. A sort of back-to-back seating arrangement, with Mass Will walking from one end to the next to instruct us. I don't recall that he had anyone else to assist him.

On a Sunday, the name 'school' would come up again. But this was a different type of school though. At church there was no khaki uniform, no strap or whips for beating, no shouting, no break or lunch times and we carried no bags or writing slates. This was called "Sunday School". It was held for just one hour, from 9:30am to 10:30am. The only book we opened was the Bible and all the words and stories came from it. There were much fewer children in Sunday school. The main lessons were set around a "Golden Text", or memory gem, which we tried to memorise and then recall for the teacher each week. So, for example, the Golden Text could be: Proverbs 22:6 says "Train up a child in the way he should go, and when he is old, he will not depart from it".

The Sunday school teacher always seemed to be happy when any of us in the class showed self-confidence and when we could repeat the Golden Text from the Bible lesson clearly and fully. As the teacher for the adult Sunday school class, my mother would always make time on a Saturday evening to read over her lesson ahead of the coming Sunday mornings. I would often take a seat next to her. Sometimes I just watched and listened as she read from pages in the Bible. She had always said that if I heard a word or phrase that I did not understand then I should tell her. When I asked, she would take her time to explain the words and their meaning to me in ways I could understand so by the time of my class on Sunday morning, I would always feel confident to read, recite the Golden Text and to ask questions. I have often said that my mother tended to always behave in ways with me that I never witnessed from other children and their mothers. For one thing, I cannot recall having heard the mother of any of my childhood playmates reading to them. My mother liked to sit down and read with me. Our main book was her Bible and the American Church of God Sankey (Song Book). As a result, I was able to develop a good understanding of what I was reading.

In Sunday school the teacher would call on those children who actively recite the Golden Text and could understand and explain its intent or meaning. But only one class was maintained. This was in contrast to the normal school, where teachers would separate the large class of children according to some measure of abilities. The more active and able ones would be streamed in two rows on one side of the classroom, with the others told to sit in the second group of two or three rows behind. In my six years at the Sandy Bay Primary/All-Age School, I honestly cannot recall any more than a small number of children from our district being streamed in the first or 'A' group. It always seemed that very few from the district sat in either of the first two front rows.

This picture at school of a less than equitable distribution of children from the district in the 'A' and 'B' streams has persisted down many generations. Children from the two communities never mixed well during my childhood years and a real sense of enmity was always on show. As a child and even later in my life, I have heard many unflattering remarks that cast most people from the district as at best, being largely illiterate, and worse, dunce, in the main. Of course, insults can cause deep injury to a person's feelings, and this laid at the root of many fights and altercations between our rival school groups. Often times the fights that started in the school yard would spill over to streets further away from the school grounds and some parents would intervene and insist that their injured child exact vengeance upon their Mount Pelier antagonists. This had made for many confrontations between parents during those childhood years, with some parents coming down the hill, stirred by anger from fights and rough justice meted out against their children. Many of those children who often got drawn into fights were very rarely devoted to the basics of learning to read or to write. They became reputed fighters and of course, teachers in any school would always isolate those who they labelled as disruptive during their class. This is in part where so many children from the district became lost to the world of formal schooling at such an early age and stage of their life. Many from the district never recovered from those difficult school years at Sandy Bay.

But as far as Sunday school class went, we were all from the same district and we all sat together, without streams or ranks. Also, we never stayed inside the main church building for our class but instead, we would be taken outside to a cool area under a breadfruit tree in the churchyard and there each child would be asked to find a smooth rock or piece of wood on which to sit. We always sat in a semi-circular formation. Without the rows of benches outside, the children who showed more interest would somehow find themselves towards the front of the group and that was a quite natural process of selection. Those that were not so actively involved or interested would still remain in the semi-circle as the teacher read from the Bible and try to explain the meanings of words and phrases to us. At the end of our one-hour session a bell would sound and all the different age-based classes would quickly be reassembled inside the church building. The person appointed to be the Sunday School Superintendent would then take over and conduct a short class-by-class review on the topic and detail of their lesson. I have always felt that the greatest satisfaction for a Sunday school teacher was in seeing the children they taught displaying self-confidence when called upon to say what they had learned. The Superintendent would often ask a whole class to recite together the topic of their lesson and the Golden Text or memory verse. There were never many hands raised voluntarily to give answers to the review questions. But you can guess that my little hands would always be flying up to head up the scanty race to give an answer. Because of my delight to go to church each Sunday, the label, "Church Boy", would follow me, both at basic and then primary school and also into casual fun and play with relatives or strangers in our open grass yard at home. I was never certain as to whether the label was meant for a compliment or an insult.

On reflection, I have often thought that sometimes the attitudes and impressions we form about each other from even such early years do endure and can get so deeply rooted so as to generate misplaced stereotypes and false impressions about people and their community. Many of the children, and perhaps more so boys, who became alienated from formal learning at an early primary school stage seemed also to be among those who were least interested in Sunday school and by their early teen years would stop attending church altogether.

The Word of God in Scriptures is not always so easy to read or to understand. So just try to imagine how challenging it would be in future years for those adults in the church who had not managed to learn the basics of reading and writing, to then grow in self-confidence from reading and understanding their Bible. To be able to read God's Word, at a basic level at the very least, must be encouraged as an essential part of the journey and armour of faith. Hearing the Word of God being read and interpreted by a third person can be helpful. But just imagine how much more enriched a person could be when they are able to open their Bible and read over the words in their own time and space for themselves. Hence the importance of Sunday school in the very early unfolding years of young lives. It was always a special treat during the seasons of Christmas and Easter for our Sunday school teacher to prepare prizes and surprises for the class. I recalled winning picture books on the life of heroic Bible characters such as king David, Samson, Jacob and Esau, Joseph, Jonah, Daniel and his three Hebrew friends, Moses and Joshua among many others. The more books I got simply motivated me to read about the workings of the Spirit of God in the people who pleased Him. The more I read the more I became familiar with some of the simpler stories of the Bible and even when the actual details would fade from me many years later, their moral flavour would still remain in my memory.

The first Sunday school teacher that I remember was Sister Patsy. This was her locally known 'pet name' as I found out many years later, and that her given name was actually Joan Evans. She taught the primary age group Sunday school class. The youngest group was called the 'Beginners' class, next was the Juniors and then our age would have been in the range of nine to eleven years old. Sis. Patsy was young and vibrant, likely in her teen years, as I recall. She smiled easily as she organised us to sit around her in a semicircle. She may have sat on a low wooden stool under the outdoor shade of a breadfruit tree in the churchyard. A small exercise book was used for the class register and when she called my name I always answered quickly with a shout of, 'present teacher'. This may have been the same response that I gave at the basic school with Mass Will' and then at the Sandy Bay primary school. Because, besides the fact that this was on a Sunday, I would have treated Sunday mornings as though I was present in a class at normal school. But we never referred to Sis. Patsy as our "church Sister", as the adults would do when they interrupted her for whatever reason. We just addressed her as "Miss", when we were invited to raise our hands to respond to questions during the lesson. So, for example, when she taught us about Joseph and his brothers in Egypt, my hand would be among the first to shoot up with an answer that begins with 'I know, miss' or' 'me miss'.

I don't remember the number of years that we were in her class. It may have been more than just one year and I say this because I think that it was unlike the annual progression into a new class at our primary school at Sandy Bay. There we would move to a new classroom every September. All the Sunday school classes included mixed age ranges of say, three years old up to six years and, in any case I cannot recall moving into the class of any other Sunday school teacher.

In some strange ways I am able to remember the voice tone and smile of Sister Patsy. She never shouted at any of us, nor slapped any of us in the class. Her eyes were always sweeping around the sitting cluster of our small bodies as she discussed the subject and the main story from the lesson with us. Maybe I remembered so much about Sister Patsy because she used to call me her 'assistant', and anytime she was called away from the class or if she had to go inside the church building for any reason, she would always call me to come and stand at the front in her stead. She would give the Bible to me, opening to the page that I was reading from. The Bible would fill both my hands but I always tried to do as Sister Patsy asked. I was able to read the text out aloud before the class, and maybe even continue with the discussion or questions that she had started. When the Sunday school time was over, after one hour, our class would be shepherded to cluster together on the front benches in the church. It was then that another person would come to stand in front of the church and begin the "Sunday school" classes review, on a class-by-class basis. The whole process would take only about 15-20 minutes, moving from the youngest class first and continuing through to the oldest adult-class that my mother taught. The reviewer would begin by asking, what was the subject of the lesson that the class covered? I suppose this process was the test of whether we had learnt or understood anything from the one-hour lesson. Sister Patsy and all the other teachers could not intervene at this time. They had to sit aside and observe as somebody else tested the fruit of their one-hour labour in the Scriptures. Inside the church we sat on long benches, each holding nine or ten of us, as the whole class. For some reason I would always be seated at the end of the bench. I liked this part of the process in much the same way that I liked to be in Sister Patsy's class. Whatever question the reviewer asked, I would always have a quick answer to offer. The questions were related to the subject that we had covered. Sometimes they would ask the whole class to repeat aloud, all together, the topic of the lesson and the verse of the Golden Text. My mother always called this the "Memory Verse", when we talked about it on the Saturday evening prior to each Sunday. So, for example, the topic of the lesson might be, "David slew Goliath." During the lesson Sis. Patsy would have drilled us into reciting together those words in the same order. We would repeat this for five or six times and at different times during the one-hour lesson. Perhaps at the very beginning when Sister Patsy began the class and again when she read out the story of the fight between David and Goliath from the Scriptures of the Old Testament portion of the Bible. The New Testament words were easier to read and understand for me as a child because the words were much like those in the reading books at normal school, but the best fighting characters and their wonderful stories were in the Old Testament. Many of the words in the Old Testament were so much more difficult for us to pronounce and understand fully. For one thing many of the names for the thirty-nine different books that comprised the Old Testament were completely strange to us. For example, the first five books of the Old Testament are called: Genesis, Exodus, Leviticus, Numbers and Deuteronomy. Except for the one named Numbers, all the others would be totally unfamiliar to us as children, and perhaps more so to those children in our class who didn't have parents who attended church or read from the Bible to them at home. Words or titles like 'Leviticus' or 'Deuteronomy', for example, may never have come to the hearing of a child of our age, except for in the church building. I don't know how many adults can even remember these Bible names and words after the church service ended.

One of the great skills that Sister Patsy had and used for teaching us was that she loved to tell us about the goodness of God and Jesus and that of the Holy Ghost. I think that she just liked to talk about God and things connected to God and she wanted us to love these names also. My mother had already helped me to get some level of understanding of these names. They were names familiar to anyone who liked to read the Bible. My mother always reads her Bible on a Saturday evening. Sunday, the first day of the week by modern calendar, was our day of worship. We followed all the teachings and practices of the apostles in this. During a service, we would be asked to open the Bible almost all of the time. At the beginning of a service, one of the adult members would go up to the high pulpit to say words of welcome and greetings. They would lead us into offering up thanks and praise to God for keeping all of us alive for another week. We would sing together from the hymnal or songbook. The Bible would be the next book opened. They would say which Book of the Bible we should turn to, and then read together the portion of the selected Scripture. This first activity was called the morning devotion. It was always the opening session of a service in the church. The Sunday school session would be the next activity, as each child and adult would be allotted to go to a class and this was based on age groups. After the Sunday school was through, there would next be the time when the Sunday School Superintendent would stand up to read off the details of the total number of persons present in Sunday school, the offering collected by each class with confirmation of the amounts recorded for the week, in total.

The Divine Worship segment would start after a brief interlude used to sing some choruses. My mother always said that this part of the service was the most important. In some ways, this part of the service brought about a level of serious focus upon the things of God that are recorded in the Scriptures. At this time the younger children would be told to sit quietly, with no movement in or out of the building. This final segment of the service was where the pastor came to the pulpit. They would open the Bible again and deliver their preaching or sermon. This would continue for at least one hour up to the point when the pastor completed his sermon and we all stood for a closing prayer, with the congregation then asked to join in pronouncing the closing benediction. It went something like," *And now may the saving grace of our Lord and Saviour Jesus Christ, the love of God the Father, in full fellowship of the Holy Spirit, the Comforter. May He rest, remain and abide with us all, now and forever, Amen."*

The interest generated during Sunday school would continue into a regular Monday evening church service where young persons would again be involved with Bible reading and reciting, singing and performing. I don't recall missing many Sunday-school classes and I would have missed even less Monday evening YPE (Young People's Endeavour), and where we would repeat the national church pledge from the Bible from part of a verse in Zachariah 4:6, "Not by might, nor by power but by my spirit, saith the Lord of hosts." There was also a national church motto which said, "Together we aspire, together we achieve." The Monday evenings meetings continued to stick in my memory for many years thereafter for the songs and recitations especially. It was because for those meetings that I would collect and perform a number of songs, poems, nursery rhymes and verses. I was always given the opportunity to be involved in the activity programme and this moulded my self confidence in the ability to understand and memorise written material quickly. I especially enjoyed ministry in songs and in acting out skits and short pieces of drama or plays, taken from Bible stories. I was often called upon to recite poems, rhymes and recitations. It was through such programmes in the church that I had my first memory of travelling from the district to areas beyond the primary school at Sandy Bay. The names of some of the other New Testament churches became familiar from events like rallies and singing concerts. There were neighbouring place names such as Pondside, Cascade, Claremont, Retrieve, Lucea and Askenish, among others that our church visited and supported. Sometimes I would be taken along by adults to render an item such as a song. I was taught to always give a low standing bow before I started to sing or to recite. My mother kept me with a supply of new songs and verses. Sometimes my acts would amuse the watching congregation. I remember one particular short poem, where I had to finish with a motion of bulging and popping out my eyes wide open. It went something like this:

> I am a little man
>
> Just dropped from the sky
>
> Drop in a hog sty
>
> Dirty up my tie
>
> And if you think is a lie

Just look into my eyes!

(With me using my fingers to bulge the eyes wide open to finish)!

Or this one as I recall it:

I have two eyes, but one tongue

I have two ears, but one tongue

I have two hands, but one tongue

I have two feet, but one tongue

So, members; pastors; deacons

Remember to watch your tongue!

But in so far as performances went perhaps the funniest of all the verses, skits and recitations that I can remember was one that had not a single spoken word at all! All I was asked to do was go up on the pulpit in the normal way, give my bow and take my position to perform. Only that I never spoke a single word even as I stood up there. I think that one had never been performed before the church before. My mother helped to prepare me. She had said that I should just stand and then begin to count in my head up to ten. I would then give a nod at the end and then walk right down again. Now it worked because people who knew of my acts in the church would know that I didn't get stage fright so easily and to the point of forgetting all the words. I had gone up and stood beside the pulpit many times before to give songs, play a role in a skit or short character plays without forgetting my lines. But in that wordless recitation, some in the watching congregation would have expected some words to come out. And when none was forthcoming there were some stirring on the benches, others looking around for my mother to come to my rescue and remind me of the words that they think I had forgotten. But when they saw that I was not panicked, and I then bowed in the usual way of ending and walked back to my seat, then they would have realised that it was all part of the act! Many years after we had left the district, and I had returned to visit the area and attended the church, a few people would still remind me of that recitation without words and would still muse at the performance of that one.

Chapter Nine
Childhood Baptism

I was included among a sizeable group of young and older teenagers, young persons and some adults who were invited to accept water baptism. This offer came after the sixth evening of week-long evangelistic or crusade meetings at our church. These meetings were very different to the usual Sunday and weekday meetings. During what members called 'Crusade Week', all routine meetings in our church would be cancelled for that week. Local people in the community would refer to the week as a 'Church of God Crusade'. These were open public meetings that had become a major part of a church year, and where the purpose was to draw and concentrate attention on people who were still living for the world instead of for the sovereign ruler, God their creator. It was an opportune time to evangelise and remind the unsaved that this world would not continue to exist forever and that their own days on the earth can be cut off by God at any moment. Beyond death of the mortal body, the unchanging message of the New Testament gospels made the promise that only those who accept Jesus Christ as their personal Saviour and Lord over their destiny, will be saved from eternal condemnation in the judgement and fire of eternal torment in hell. Members of the church would look to the crusade as a special week for preaching that was planned by the pastor for the harvesting of yet unsaved souls. Every person in our small district who was not already saved would get the opportunity to attend and hear the 'Good News' of the gospel message. They would be invited to confess Jesus as Saviour and repent before coming into fellowship with existing members at the church.

I am not able to recall any such type of evangelistic or revivalist week of service at the church at any time previous to that one. But there would most likely have been others like it; I just cannot recall anything even similar from before the occasion of my baptism. In any case crusades were a very well-established tradition for a New Testament Church of God to plan and host evangelistic meetings and these would not have changed much from previous generations. The main feature for the week was that we had a visiting preacher, meaning that they would not be our regular pastor but came from outside our community. They would not be attached to any of the familiar churches in the areas that we already knew. I don't remember all the details but an announcement would likely have been made to the congregation in advance to the dates by our own church pastor. There may have been a large information poster or billboards made up about the event. But in any case, all the members of the church were asked to spread and publish the news of the upcoming week of meetings around the district. This was information about who the new visiting evangelist would be; his name, and the number of evenings or nights that he would be preaching in the church. Such announcements of a visiting evangelist always brought about a rush of excitement in the community and I'm sure it had aroused the same flurry of anticipation in other people attending the church, because the best of these speakers came packed with charisma, powerful voice, stories of sinners coming to repentance and sharp words of rebuke for those who will not accept Jesus Christ in their lives.

At the close of the week of crusade meetings, a number of persons who heard and accepted the gospel message, would walk to the altar and agreed to be baptised. It was said that some of the older candidates may have been returning to the church after backsliding from a previous baptism. According to my mother, they had 'turned back,' having previously made a start to follow Christ. I may have been one of the younger candidates in that group accepting water baptism. But just how much I would have understood there and then about the commitment to Christ in water baptism I really don't know. I suspect that I would not have understood very much about the real meaning of either my life or of the eternal love of God at that age and stage. As I recall, very little guidance or support would have existed, either inside of the church or on the outside, to help young children understand the things of the Spirit. I would have been very familiar with words such as 'sin and iniquity,' because these were spoken about by my mother at home, and read out in Sunday school and, preached from the pulpit. I knew that it was a sin to disobey my mother or to use 'bad words' and tell lies. That it was sin to be involved in sexual relations unless you were married. All of these acts of sins were already familiar to me. But I might not have understood at my age that it was also a sin if I did not give praise and worship to God alone every day.

I had not seen any Bible that was specifically printed and published for children during my early years as a matter of fact. As far as I was aware during my childhood in the church, there was only one version of the Holy Bible published. I honestly thought that adults alone bought copies of it, if they were able to read. I had been raised in the church from my earliest childhood. My mother was a great reader and she helped me to read through passages of her copy of the Bible and when I did not understand a portion of text, she would help me. I could read and understand most of the words on the pages but had no real sense of the deeper spiritual truths being conveyed by the books of Moses or the letters from Paul, for example. From reading through passages of the New Testament books of the Bible, I had got used to seeing the word 'baptism'. I had never been to any baptism service anywhere before my own and so had no real understanding of its spiritual symbolism or public statement.

I can recall reading about the colourful character of John the Baptist in the four gospel accounts at the beginning of the New Testament Scriptures. John had certainly baptised many people in the River Jordan and ministered to Jesus before he was killed by a wicked king. But it was also my understanding that John's main work was to call Jewish people to repentance. After preaching the gospel to them and admonished them about turning away from the commands of God, John would call them to change from their fallen and sinful ways, and offered water baptism to any who came by their free will. John had made clear this he was not the expected Messiah promised to Israel by God. But he was the forerunner, sent to make the way clear for Jesus the Saviour, and who already present amongst them in a body of human flesh. So I had some early idea of just what water baptism should be about. I don't know whether each and every other new convert also understood it in this same way. I don't know whether any one of them thought that baptism was the only act that was necessary to secure a place in God's promised kingdom of heaven.

It seem even more important that a child candidate for water baptism should be helped to understand that the act of their baptism do not mean that you would go to heaven. It was one of the misunderstandings that I had harboured at that time. I would have better understood the explanation that baptism was merely a public display of a changed attitude towards God and fellow men. Children especially should always be given clear and meaningful guidance and counselling, even as the convicting power of the Holy Spirit work inside them to secure young souls unto God. The soul of the child is as valued by God as every other. Yet a younger child may need sufficient time to come to a clear understanding of just who God is and also of the workings of the Spirit and free will in all godly things. Each person is encouraged by the gospel message to take responsibility for their own soul. Hence, even a child must be guided to understand both the need for the redemption of the soul and also for God's favour of grace after repentance and baptism. If the child or an adult for that matter have not yet understand the essence of God and the place of public water baptism, then they might not give due honour to the baptismal pledge. Hence the baptised child who has not yet developed that understanding will remain vulnerable to the attacks and temptation by the world and the desires in their flesh.

I believe the pastor at that time of my childhood baptism was named Pastor Ashbourn Allen. He followed immediately behind Pastor Conrod Grant. A pastor was generally appointed to lead a congregation by the National Island Office of the church in Kingston and would have worked in maintaining membership and the continuation of that local church. They would have been directed to lead in a godly shepherd-like way and to always act under the counsel of the Holy Spirit. They would have been instructed to minister within the tenets of the 'Articles of Faith and Practices', as declared and approved by the International Church of God Office in Cleveland, Tennessee. Pastors appointed to a local New Testament church were probably encouraged to initiate ministry that yielded new converts for baptisms and increase membership for the body of Christ. As a child I might not have known that the mere act of baptism did not amount to the saving of my soul, or that baptism should confirm a deeper inner conviction to grow in the Christian faith. Hence, a new pastor sent into a local church should quickly try to recognise the need of those who sit in front of them every Sunday. For most pastors, it takes time before they begin understand the spiritual needs in the church. It is only after this becomes clear that they can really begin to promote better understanding in the things of God. The recognition of the need for spiritual light should always be at the forefront of the mind of every church leader. Ultimately it is the new converts' understanding of baptism and the working of God's saving grace in their life that matters. Hence, if I do not understand the things of God then I will not likely endure to the end.

CHAPTER TEN
Church Membership

I had been active in attendance and participation in the church from childhood, but not counted as a member. Membership and the formal confirmation of fellowship, have always been set aside for those people who accept water baptism. This is what many local people refer to as 'joining the church'. I had taken part in all the events that were available to children in the church. I did not assume my first appointed position as a member of the church until shortly after my childhood water baptism when I was appointed to serve as the assistant to the Sunday School Superintendent, and who was a Bro France Hayles, for that time. I was at primary/All-Age school in Sandy Bay. On occasions when the Superintendent was not present at church on a Sunday morning, I would occupy the seat at a corner table and from where I received and recorded information for the number of persons attending each Sunday school class and the amount of offering collected. I would record the information in a exercise book labelled 'Weekly Sunday School Minutes', and at the time appointed for the Sunday School Superintendent I would stand and read the information aloud to the congregation. Following the reading of those Minutes, a senior member would then proceed to ask whether the information provided a accurate record of the foregoing. At that point it required one member raise their hand and to say the words, 'I accept the Minutes as a true record.' Another member would then say, 'I second that.' The Minutes would then be approved and thereafter be treated as part of the official record required of the church. This was the beginning of my service to the church. It would be almost forty years before I was again elected into a second position of service in my childhood family church.

As a member of the church I often heard the two words, "brotherly love and sisterly love." They would be repeated very often during my childhood years. People in the church didn't speak about the Bible's meaning of these words. They were common everyday words and could even be in songs played on the radio. I can recall many phrases that encouraged people to live in love and unity, as brothers and sisters on our island. Whenever my mother explained the meaning of brotherly and sisterly love to me, she would speak in the context of believers living together for God and meeting up together to hold services as we did, to pray and offer thanks through Jesus Christ. But sometimes we would also hold meetings outside of the building in places on the street or at the home of one of the members. A non-member could just walk into the church during a service and join in the singing and worship. That was a voluntary or free willed choice that anyone could make. This was the first level of togetherness of like-minded Christian believers. But it could also get much deeper and closer than that between church bothers and sisters. There were times and occasions when a member of the church would face real challenges in their own life or, among their children or in their wider family. They would ask the pastor or other senior or older members of the church to pray for a situation or for the person in question. I can recall the occasion when one sister in the church had a real situation to deal with. This concerned one of her sons, who was arrested by the police for some alleged offence. I don't know what his offence was, but I remember that a police car from the station at Sandy Bay was present one Sunday morning. The armed uniformed officers went into the house of the family and her son was taken out in handcuffs behind his back. His mother was senior, by her age, in the church and she duly collapsed to the ground, weeping and pleading to God in her son's cause. The entire district seemed to be taken by surprise that morning, with onlookers crowding into the open yard before the house. The chattering and questioning spread amongst some while other people just standing around quietly in close proximity, even after the police vehicle had left with her son. I guess people were just trying to find out what crime her son had committed and the charges made by the police. Yet others just added speculation and village hearsay, even to the point of some declaring their own judgement of guilt or innocence. When the mother arrived at the church service that morning other members rallied around her, prayed and spoke words of encouragement to her heart. After the day's service was over, there were other members of the church who would offer comfort and talked further with her. Later during that same Sunday evening, I can recall that a group of members again went to the house and offered more prayers. They were all fellow believers together, trying to share the burden of another member of the church in their time of trouble.

My mother had often said that the cares and troubles of this world would continue long, but would not be forever. Other people in the church also made several repeats of that same expression. They share a sense of being Christian pilgrims and strangers on the earth together. They believed the Word of God that there would come a day when the trials of life will come to an end. It was in this belief that members of the church would so often meet together. It gave them the sense of sharing something eternally valuable to the soul. They would speak of themselves as travelling on a journey with Jesus Christ, the Son of God, and that this would end in a glorious day. It was the sense of sharing a common aim and spiritual destiny which undergird the Christian hope of being accepted into the eternal presence of God in heaven. Sometimes that bond of unity also meant that believers shared many common challenges and tribulations, personal persecutions and temptations. Hence, this is why my mother always said that believers should walk and stay close together as sisters and brothers for God. Those meeting together each week were members of the family of God. They were together in the same congregation and sharing the same hope of making it into the presence of God.

In so far as I am able to recall the different pastors appointed to lead the members of our church from around the time of my primary years, none surpassed the name of the Blairs'. There were three pastors that I can recall clearly and of those, two were young men aged in their mid-20's when they first came to lead the church. The first of these was Pastor Roy Owen, and he was followed in a few years by Pastor Conrod Grant. In the case of the former, I can remember that he liked to sing even as he made his approach to the pulpit each Sunday. In the case of the latter, I don't remember him ever singing in church, but he left a more lasting memory for me because of his family. When Pastor Conrod Grant came to our church, I believe that a house was rented for him to live in the area. I recall that an older brother named Phillip accompanied him at first. But at some time after that, there were two younger sisters, named Pearl and Daisy, who would often visit him. One of the sisters would later get married to a local man and took up permanent residence in the district. The third that I can remember was called Pastor Ashbourn Allen. He was the serving pastor at the time when we left the district for England. He would later marry a local sister in the church and continued to pastor for some time afterward.

CHAPTER ELEVEN
A Church In The Mother Country

It was during Pastor Allen's time at the church that my mother decided to return to England. She had lived there twenty years before. But returned home in some haste in order to protect the six older children, whom she had left behind with grandma Estry. So this would be a second time around for her. During the first settlement in England, she had taken up membership at a New Testament church denomination established by migrating Jamaicans in the town of Walsall, in the English West Midlands. The contrast between the environs we had left and the place where we arrived could not have been any more marked. Just to take a Sunday as an example, it became obvious that this day was not treated as sacred for rest or worship. Most of the population of Walsall just seemed to continue in their regular activities, regardless of the day. In fact, most people went out to work and those not going out to work simply spent the day occupied by sporting, music or social events. The very air we breadth in the town always seem to be mixed with dark billowing smoke that came out from housetop chimneys and vents. The door of bars, pubs, drinking houses and clubs remained open throughout Sunday. But perhaps the greatest shock to my system was the absence of anything in the area that conveyed the sound of church or worship on a Sunday morning. I cannot ever recall hearing the sound of singing or hand clapping from a church at any time in that town where we lived for so many years. There was no intruding sound of drum beating, bass guitar stumming or speaker boxes turned up anywhere on a Sunday morning. Unlike our district in Jamaica, there was instead a strict adherence to legal limits on noise levels. England and the rest of the United Kingdom of Scotland, Wales, Northern Island and elsewhere all established and maintained strict noise abatement laws. When and where this level was breached, be it by places of public worship or at a private residence, the police would most certainly be summoned to step in and do the bidding of Her Majesty's court services. Immigrant communities learned these limits quickly and took seriously the object lesson of when in Rome, we must do as Romans do.

As a child accustomed to a close tie between home and the church, I could be forgiven for feeling like a small fish taken out from its familiar water. That was largely how I came to feel in the early days in the English town of Walsall. I would come to accept that change was not in or by itself a bad thing. But even so, there are some times where the change of your environment can be deeply unsettling. The impression which had developed in my head about the treatment of a Sunday morning was to be shattered, on the very continent where the apostles that I read about in the New Testament Bible ministered the teaching and preaching of the gospel message started by Jesus Christ. The distance from England to Rome (in Italy) was much less than it was from Palestine to Rome. So in the naïve thinking of a child, I could be forgiven for making assumptions that to be closer to Rome would mean being closer to the heart of Christianity. But it was not proving to be so for me.

It was sometime during my secondary school years and taking Religious Education as a subject that I remember reading about a church led by the well-known English evangelical preacher named Charles Spurgeon. He had pastored the Metropolitan Tabernacle Baptist church somewhere in East London. That was a time when hundreds of worshippers attended his Sunday morning meetings. By any measure, that was a church to rival the biggest American Evangelist Ministries today. That blast from England's Christian past is readily backed up by observing the imposing size of some of the oldest Anglican, Methodist and Roman Catholic Church buildings in old towns like Walsall. I had always assumed that there must have been past days when great numbers attended and participated in public worship across the length and breadth of the Kingdom. But of course, much more time given to Christian worship in the days when Charles Spurgeon was on fire for God, than today. Those days have passed to the pages of history and many grand church buildings have since trended into emptiness and dereliction. While those relics of the past stand as the evidence of changes in the ways of life for many Christian nations, it is not the sort of change that my mother would join in to celebrate. Because for her this meant a change from the ways of living for God to other contrary lifestyles. Yet the naked truth is that weekly Christian worship has been steadily drifting away from public view in all the countries of Europe for more than a century to now.

But that is truly amazing when one stops to consider that Christianity itself had found its way to Rome in Italy at the very start of the first century of Jesus Christ. The Scriptures tell of this history through the books of the New Testament. From an initial group of twelve disciples, and who later graduated to bold and brave apostles, the narrative of Christianity tells of their work to spread the teachings of faith and truth in God. Beginning with the grandstanding of the church at Rome, the capital city of a great and vast military empire, successive generations of evangelizing Christians have spread the name of Jesus Christ to every nation, moving on sea and over land. Rome had been a seat of great military might and power and the 'universal' Roman Catholic Church flourished as the leader of Western Christianity up to the middle years of the 1500's when some core beliefs and religious practices were challenged from within.

A new dissenting Christian movement called 'Protestantism', initiated a second division of the Catholic Church and thereafter, disagreements and separation from within this emerging western Christian movement would become commonplace. In our religious education classes in secondary school, there were many books in the library with pictures of grand looking men under the names such as Martin Luther, John Wesley, John Calvin, John Knox and others. Those were the most esteemed leaders of the Protestantism which became established in countries such as England, France, Germany, Holland, as well as in other places. The only religious books that did not bear the names of these new leaders of Western Christianity was the Holy Bible. It is noteworthy also that in the small matter of five hundred years following the great split of the Roman Catholic Church, the previous high number of Lutheran, Wesleyan, Methodist, Presbyterian and Baptist churches on main streets in towns like Walsall have dwindled down to just a few. Gradually, the names of many grand European men and the Christian churches established in their names have quietly disappeared from public view.

In part this condition also reflected the cold rejection of arriving black immigrants from their worship and membership in the years following the Second World War when the first generation of black Christians bravely knocked on their doors. This was one of the reasons why many Jamaican Christians sought to establish their own 'Americanised' brand of Pentecostal Christian churches. I say 'Americanized' because while the number of prominent European Christian missionaries fell away after the Second World War the Americans prospered in leading new Pentecostal evangelism work in many predominantly black nations in the Caribbean. The point I am making is that the doors of many Christian churches were closed to incoming black immigrants in England in the 1940s and 50s especially. Yet many black people had already become accustomed to the American brand of Pentecostal worship at home in Jamaica and elsewhere throughout the English-speaking colonised islands. So, in reaching England, black migrants simply reverted to re-establishing their familiar American registered churches and planted new branches in towns like Walsall, Wolverhampton and elsewhere. It is worth noting also that among the migrating families there could be found both men and women who were baptised into their rural or town churches on the islands, with some leaving senior positions as active ministers, deacons and officers. Promptly, they set about the re-creation of their home denominations in the 'Mother Country'. The American church leaders were gifted with new and unexpected opportunities to add to their branded denominations and churches after Britain opened its doors to large scaled job seeking black immigrants. This was really how churches such as the New Testament Church of God became planted and embedded in England from the 1950s. They introduced new approaches to free styled Pentecostalism to England. They found new ways to seek out lost souls, reaching the unconverted, preaching the message of the Good News by the power of God that led to salvation, and in teaching to strengthen Christian conviction and deepen discipleship.

Traditional English churches such as the one led by Charles Spurgeon would become less prominent even as the churches established by black immigrants look forward to the future. So, the English had brought the older nationally sponsored denominations to Jamaica and other English held Caribbean Island colonies (Anglican, Methodist, Presbyterian, Wesleyan Holiness and Catholic). Now it was the turn of black immigrants to return their missionary favours by setting up churches in their heartland.

Chapter Twelve
One Congregation Becomes Three Churches

My mother had returned to the same town of Walsall in England. The New Testament church she had joined more than fifteen years before with other expatriate Jamaicans, was still located on its original site along the Wednesbury Road. This was just a short distance to the main shops and trade area of the town. Much time had passed since she was a member there, and no doubt many of the more familiar faces were no longer there. Several family members and friends from her home district of Cascade, and also from Mount Pelier, also made the move to Walsall during the 1950s and 60s. She lived amongst other church going migrants from nearby rural districts such as Retrieve, Pondside, Cascade and Maryland. So she had been well at home in many ways. But things and times changed. That original immigrant congregation at Wednesbury Road, which include many Hanoverian families, would later suffer internal leadership disputes and rivalries in the early 1970's while my mother was back in Jamaica. It might well be that many of her closer friends at the church left and went elsewhere with one or other of the splintered branches because on returning to Walsall a second time she did not find that original membership core at Wednesbury Road, although the church was still there.

I believe that at least three separated congregations emerged from the splitting at the Wednesbury Road church. My mother had remained in contact with several members of that original congregation during the intervening years from Jamaica and she opted to join with perhaps the smallest group. This comprised just four or five families. The nominal pastor was connected to our family. His wife was a niece to my father. Only one of the families in that small congregation was from another Caribbean island. As I recall, all the rest were Jamaicans, and mainly Hanoverians. This was a church that did not look or even felt like a church to me. I attended with my mother for some months. But it didn't grab me as a church. For one thing it was a church without a building that was dedicated for worship. We met in an open hall rented for just a few hours each Sunday morning. There was no pulpit or lantern used, no choir, drums or microphones. The leader, a mature Jamaican man and his wife were active as brethren at the Wednesbury Road church throughout the 1960s. In so far as I was aware, he was not formally trained for the leadership of church ministry. But like so many others he was regarded as a good and self-confident speaker from the pulpit. They had a small mini-bus and went from house to house, picking up those members who didn't own a car. My father never attended the gathering, and he never owned a car so we relied upon the drive in the minibus. The place of our worship was not designed to host church but for sports and recreation. So in the search for a place to house this small breakaway group that left the Wednesbury Road church, the leader had rented the hall for use on a Sunday morning. I don't remember what time the meetings would start or end but I do recall that we would start only when the leader had collected the small number of members, both adults and mainly children such as my brother and me. Maybe we sang hymns and well known choruses such as we were accustomed with from church in Jamaica. I don't remember any songs from the time there and again I really cannot remember any sermon by the leader of the group. I can remember though that when we were at our little district church in Jamaica each Sunday service would begin with Sunday school and then continue with singing and devotion from the Scriptures before the preacher for that day would be introduced by the meeting's moderator. There were times in Jamaica when my mother would be the moderator and sometimes, or she was asked to preach. But I really cannot recall any such structure to meetings at the break away church in Walsall, for there must have been structure of some kind. But it left no lasting impression in my memory. It could be that I had associate the idea of a church with certain mode of conduct or activity. For example, I expected Sunday school and what was called 'YPE' (Young People's Endeavour) meetings, with other daytime and evening gatherings. But in this case, none of those were present or consistent.

My mother had often repeated a verse from the Bible that said, *'For where two or three are gathered together in my name, there I am in the midst of them.'* But I am not sure that the verse should even be applied to that situation. Because I think that perhaps the most telling thing in the verse is the act of gathering, rather than the numbers. There are many millions of professed Christians across the length and breadth of the globe. Each and every one of them hold the belief that a Christian church is the possession of God Himself, and is the body of His only begotten Son, Jesus Christ. The Triune nature of God is a mystery, existing together in the eternal Father, Son and Holy Spirit. So while I believe it to be true that any number of persons can gather themselves together under the label called a church, that really is not what makes a church to become a church, according to the New Testament Scriptures. The gathering has to be done by the working of God's supernatural power in the heart of the believing participant. I don't know whether this breakaway church was in fact gathered in this way because, after a time, I believe it closed. With God in the midst of a gathering, I think there can be no failing because He never fails.

My mother had a heart for giving thanks and worship to God and I think that throughout her own life she was consistently joined in the fellowship of a church. It may have been upsetting for her to have first joined the church at Wednesbury Road, and then to return to the breakaway group that didn't operate for very long. I don't remember whether she had ever considered accompanying my father to the Baptist Church he attended. But then she had often remarked that Baptist meetings were not lively! The greater exuberance in worship, singing and shouting was more to her personal taste. So even when she was at what seemed to be a loose end in her faith, she quickly took the decision to move again to the second group that had also been formed after the Wednesbury Road break away.

I really have no idea as to why she never appeared to consider rejoining in fellowship with that original church. But she opted instead to continue with the second group, known as the United Church of God. This was first located on Stafford Street in Walsall and not all that far away from the original church at Wednesbury Road. The leader, in this case, was an altogether different sort of character. For one thing, this leader had acquired formal credentials as a minister. He had been one of the younger supporting ministers at Wednesbury Road. Maybe he had simply stepped out into his calling to lead a church, but I really don't know. A much more sizeable group went with him to form the 'United Church of God', and today that church is back in the fold of the New Testament Church of God, and continue to operate from the location at Chuckery Road in Walsall. I am not altogether certain of the amount of time that had elapsed between the closing of the first group and my mother joining this second group. But I can recall that I did not join their number. In the first group I was not more than a young teenage boy who attended with my mother and one older brother. I was never re-baptised or given membership in that group. I may have got to age fourteen by this time. I was also at comprehensive school in Rushall, another town near Walsall. I had become deeply engrossed in playing Sunday League junior football during the autumn and winter months. During the spring and summer months it was cricket that grabbed my attention. So somewhere between those two English national sporting pastimes, church attendance fell away through a crack. It would not be retrieved again until many years thereafter.

My mother continued in her weekly Sunday attendance at the United Church of God when they relocate from Stafford Street to Chuckery Road. I must have also attended with her at some times. I became familiar with the pastor and with several members of that church. I had a number of cousins who attended also. But I don't recall any deeper involvement with the group except for the occasional visits and these mainly were when social family events like gospel music concerts or other events involving serving food and fundraising. When viewed from their years of meeting then there must have been some greater degree of leadership structure at the second church. In time they came to acquire a building and operated as an independent religious organisation. I don't know much about what would be required to establish a group that was gathered as a registered church. But I would expect that at the very least there would be the all important consideration of whether God the Father had first ordains a thing to happen, and then whether Jesus Christ approves it and, if the Holy Spirit sustains it. God sent His Son, Jesus into the world via ancient Palestine more than 2000 plus years ago. All Christian churches profess to believe and accept that as a fact. The life and work of Jesus was to deliver the will of God the Father in setting the world free from the stronghold established by Satan. That mission was successfully accomplished in his total obedience to the Father's will. He defeated Satan at the cross on Calvary, taking away the fear and sting of death held over us when he died and was then resurrected in the power of God, to live again eternally. It is the Holy Spirit that attests to the life and works of Jesus and it is that same spirit that gathers true believers together in a Christian church. So if the Holy Spirit was not involved in the gathering together of any grouping who profess to meet in the name of Jesus, then strictly speaking they should not be called a 'Christian' church.

A second thing to consider would be to give the grouping a name, a legal identity or status. It has often been cited in the history of the New Testament Church of God in Jamaica, that when the American missionaries first came to the island in the early years of the 1900s, they had intended to operate under the name 'Church of God', as it was legally registered at its base in Cleveland, Tennessee. But in some peculiar and mixed up way, that name ('Church of God'), was found to already be registered and was in use on the island, under another denomination. I haste to imagine the confusion that there must have been when this was discovered. Since that name was already taken legally and those who registered it had no intention of surrendering it to rival missionaries. So that second matter to consider for any group, the legal identity of a religious gathering, is also important.

The new church moved quickly to establish itself as a fully-fledged Pentecostal Christian church. They met on Sunday mornings, held Sunday school before Divine Worship and preaching. My mother also went out to meetings on Sunday evenings. They organised Bible Study, fasting services, revival and evangelistic and mission work. The leading minister would visit our house from time to time. He didn't really speak with all of us present in the house, but just with my mother and she would direct him into the living room of our house where they would talk and perhaps pray. As a good testimony to the church, they continue to meet in the town up to this day.

Chapter Thirteen
A World of Sports

My secondary school days were now drawing to a close. I had done my final school exams but had no real idea as to what my future would look like. The school's Careers Officer had spoken to our class as a group about how to go about writing letters to potential employers. I had not been convinced by the army or police officers who had come in to speak with our class during our final weeks. They were promising long and bright careers but there were just too many stories of horror and distress circulating in migrant communities about bad cases of racism against black applicants to the national services and forces. I always chuckle at a question that one of my Asian classmates had asked the army officer after he got through a long presentation about new recruits. The question was in the order of, 'Sir, so is it true that the army pushes all the black soldiers to the front when they go to war?' The question had caused the pale white complexion of the officer to turn to bright red, as the whole class burst out into laughter and heckling. But there was something serious in the question and every black student had heard about this at some point. England, at the end of my secondary school years, was deeply mired in both truths and accusations of racial discrimination and overt colour prejudice against non-white citizens and residents. The headline making politicians were not always sympathetic to complaints and testimonies from victims. By natural instinct I am disposed to react and retaliate against every form of injustice and that of racism was especially cutting to me. There were certain places that I would seek to avoid because of open racism. My life would quickly become occupied with everything sports and reggae dancehall music. Weekends would become occupied playing football and cricket. The nights were for clubbing and parties. This was where many of my age headed and I followed along. For most of that time church did not feature in my day to day activities. But my mother maintained her membership and attendance. On occasions she invited us to the church. But there was no routine attendance. One year followed another and so that phase of my late teens simply slid by. Sporting prowess brought a level of excitement, according to the season, and whether in football or cricket. In some ways it was cricket, that great English team sport of eleven individuals, that provided me with a glimmer of a chance to forge a career in sports. I had become so engrossed with the sport that at one point, I was being coached by the son of George Headley, the great Jamaican batsman from two generation before. Ron Headley was often described as a stylish left-handed batsman and he had played a few test matches for the West Indies team during the 1970s. He lived in the English Midlands, and after ending his International and County Cricket career he continued to ply his skills in the less demanding semi-professional week-end leagues in England. There were different times during the summer tours by the great West Indies teams under Clive Lloyd and then Vivian Richards in the 1980s and early 90s when Ron would invite some of these world famous players to practise in the nets with us. That would really make a often damp summer become very special for me. I would have bowled a few balls to the likes of Desmond Haynes and to the late and great Malcolm Marshall. But the potential career path in that sport for me was cut off by by a ruptured ankle that hampered my effort to bowl at pace for long sessions. After missing out on the professional cricketing boat Ron had advised that the next best option for me would be to seek out opportunities to play in the semi-professional leagues, in Birmingham or elsewhere, serving as a paid club professional. But somehow, that route just didn't have any strong appeal to me and I decided to redirect my career focus elsewhere.

It was around the year 1987 that my father came to the end of his long working years in England. He had first arrived there in October 1957, joining seven of his own blood brothers and a youngest sister. With the exception of one of these brothers, they had all nested together in the Walsall area, with each in turn sponsoring their wives and, in some case the children they had left behind in Jamaica. My father had often told us stories about the many cold winters that he had passed through, working in unskilled jobs in English factories. It might have been in the year 1966 that he had returned to Jamaica with the intention of re-settling for good. But for reasons known to him and our mother he actually returned to Walsall just six months later and that seemed to have been the end for them. But somehow they managed to patch, repair and hold things together and was reconciled. They both reached their retirement age while in England. So a full thirty years after he migrated to England, our father returned home to live out his retirement years in Jamaica. He was a year older than our mother and he outlived her by almost four years when he passed-on in May 2003. Planning the family's future was always left to our mother. It was her who had set a five-year plan for our father to work in England in 1957. She had also devised a plan for our father to sponsor each of their four oldest children and then to sponsor herself to join them in Walsall with the youngest three. Their oldest child and our mother did join our father in Walsall in 1960 but thereafter the plan went out the door.

It was during these years that she had first attended the New Testament Church at Wednesbury Road, in Walsall.

Before the retirement and return of our mother and father to Jamaica, there was a visit from my oldest brother who was living with his own family in Canada and serving in the Church of God as a full-time pastor near Toronto, in Ontario Province. My brother's first visit to England would become a significant moment for me. But even for himself, I would hazard to guess that the placing of his feet on the damp soil of England for the very first time, would have evoked many deep memories of things he had both done or had refused to do in our family. It was this brother's blanket refusal to get on a ship for England way back in 1961 that triggered a double crisis for our mother and our family. Her plan had been well laid for the oldest children to move in a chain-like migration pattern, one after the other, and join up with our father in Walsall. The oldest sister had no objection to the plan and went on her way as the first in line. The next in line was this oldest brother. But he had a change of heart, rebelling against the plan and pointedly refused to get on the ship for England. So in making his first visit he may have seen a special irony in that whole situation from his own youthful days because the reason for his refusal was that he wanted to become a minister in the New Testament Church. At that youthful stage of mid-teens, he had been baptised at the church in Mount Pelier. One of his strong role models in ministry had just happened to be from the well known Blair family. A young Delbert Blair had emerged as a dynamic preacher in the New Testament Church and was appointed the overseer of the Sandy Bay district of churches. This group included the Mount Pelier church where my brother was baptised. He was zealous to serve the Lord and with the personal endorsement of Delbert Blair, he had resolutely decided that his best option would be to remain where he was at our home church. In time, his bold decision would be vindicated. He had resisted the will of our mother to make the move to England but then stuck to his gospel guns as it were and received a first appointment to pastor a small congregation at Delvesland, near Little London, in Westmoreland parish, back in the mid 1960s. During the next decades, he would progress to pastor churches in the parishes of St. Mary and St. Thomas before being transferred to the St. Ann parish. It was while at a New Testament Church of God, in St. Ann, that he accepted an invitation to visit Canada, and was later appointment to lead a church at, Edmonton, in Alberta Province. He had been pastoring in Canada for almost a decade when he came to see our parents in Walsall. He would have visited the church at Chuckery Road, attended by our mother at that time, and was invited to preach there. He would also make visits to the Wednesbury Road church. It causes me to wonder whether my brother might have also joined one of those churches in Walsall had he decided to travel to England back in 1961. But then we all accept that such speculations, while very natural for us to make, are best left in the workings of God's plan for each person's life. We can never tell just what may have been. So the timing of our brother's first visit had coincided with the retirement of our father. He had worked hard but managed to retain physical strength to enjoy an active retirement when that time had finally come in 1987. That was also the time that our mother said her own farewell to the church at Chuckery Road in Walsall. After they departed for home in Jamaica, it would be a further span of five years before she made one final visit to Walsall. She visited with friends at that church for the last time.

Chapter Fourteen
A Time For Renewal

Time passed and I would enter the path of further education and training. This led me into the broad areas of social policy and economic regeneration work. Those years from the late 1970s through to the end of Prime Minister Margaret Thatcher's leadership of the kingdom were especially challenging for immigrant communities. The plenteous work that had attracted so many individuals and families from Jamaica as well as from elsewhere in the Caribbean during the 1950s and 60s had dried up to a seep. Government and trades unions traded blows over industrial and national renewal strategies. For the first time in peacetime the level of general unemployment reached thirty-five percent of the working population and it was way more than one in three among youths. England fell into a deep economic recession and many white people decided to make black immigrants their scapegoats. It was crisis time and our

Prime Minister, the first woman to govern the kingdom, decided that she would play tough in a world of tough talking men. That was when the tabloid newspapers dubbed her as the 'Iron Lady.'

A strong movement was started to find a solution for the high rates of economic inactivity and to every community the politicians set the challenge for people to become creative and use whatever means they had to stimulate new employment opportunities. Immigrant communities had been made to settle in areas close to factories, manufacturing and coal burning plants. This was good and convenient when the demand for their unskilled labour was high during the 1950s and 60s. But things and times had changed and in the economic slump of the 1970s the lights went out in those factories. The areas closest to their locations suffered the effect of unemployment. So many people of working age in black families found themselves without work for the first time. When the few new job vacancies were published, black people made the complaint that they were being treated unfairly in the competition. Many found that in spite of their further and higher levels of technical and academic qualifications, they were not getting employed by white employers. There were also further negative knock-on effects of the racial discrimination at play in the allocation of private and public sector housing, health care, training and in social justice. From the earliest stages of my life there had always been certain things that I instinctively rebel against and acts of blatant injustices against poor and marginalised people ranks high on that list. I just cannot believe in the exclusion of another person just because you are in a position to act against them and the direct experiences of social and economic exclusion because their skin was dark went against the very essence of my nature. This was why I chose to seek work in the area of equality and social policy. As more years went by there would be focus upon the creation of future opportunities for the new generations of British born and reared black children. This was a great field of work as we contributed to the breakdown of many traditional barriers to social, education and employment opportunities for immigrant communities. It was in that line of work that the term 'regeneration' became prominent for me. The New Testament portion of the Bible made quite a number of references to this very word, but from the point of view of a spiritual renewal. It was later that I actually recognised the presence of the term in the Bible and thought it to be a touch ironic for me to have been moved from a preoccupation with social and economic regeneration and into one of spiritual application. Yet during those years I remained far and very distant from anything spiritual.

Yet in truth my work had involved opportunities to visit churches and public venues such as at Wednesbury Road and Chuckery Road, among others established in immigrant communities. In delivering presentations on prospective social and economic regeneration projects to some of these churches I would have spoken about the potential to make further use of building space to deliver adult learning and youth training programmes. Community based churches have the distinct advantage to reach many homes and families through their congregations. The church was therefore a good place through which to establish and sustain the social and economic base in immigrant communities. It was also through my work that I gained the benefit of meeting and interacting with several of the church leaders, pastors, bishops and other elder members in different denominations. There were often invitations for me to attend their Saturday or Sunday meetings from time to time and to present further information to church leaders, board meetings and conferences. I accepted some of the invitations and thereafter, continued to maintain contact. In some further cases I would also initiate and complete proposals, bids and tenders for local and central government funded projects that supported the aims of localised social and economic regeneration. That was the nature of at least part of my work. It would be many years later that I again encountered the term, 'regeneration', in the Bible, and saw both the close parallels and the differences in its meaning. During the normal course of my work, the term 'regeneration', carried with it a meaning of renewal. Following the 1950s and 1960s, for example, many old industrial manufacturing plants in British towns and cities were abandoned as the country attempted to rebuild its economy following the long years of wars and depression in Europe. Coal fuel for one thing was being replaced by gas and wind turbines and many old factory buildings and industrial machinery would become redundant. Several major geographical locations became classified social and economic regeneration zones. The structures and size of many British families had also begun to changed from the 1960s, becoming smaller, with less succession between generations taking place in family owned industrial plants and factories. So by the 1970s and 1980s there was a high stockpile of disused factories and derelict buildings, many closed and in ruin. The Margaret Thatcher led governments in those years had quickly come up with new policies to 'regenerate', old building units and clear economically viable sites and thus creating new jobs and skills in the process. That was the regeneration policy that became very familiar in my work. But what I never encountered was the reference to such a thing as 'spiritual regeneration', as appearing in the Bible. Often times the Word of God, in English translations, uses analogies and similes with material and natural objects in order to point us to a clear meaning. So, for example, the unregenerated in Scripture points to the condition of the human being who abide in a state of sin. That state can be changed, but only if the heart and mind was renewed by the power of God's Holy Spirit. A change from a style of life to please flesh, to one of seeking to please God is at the crux of my understanding of the word regeneration. Today I can see clearly the connection between my in-born and in-bred nature, which is distinctly human and flesh. This nature is not yet subject to spiritual regeneration. It is the nature we associate with the original sin and fall of Adam and Eve, in the Garden of Eden, when they showed the first selfish inclination to go after their own independent knowledge. They chose the knowledge of the devil and a life outside the daily counsel of God, their Creator. The Christian believer holds to the truth that all life came from God and that for each life, there is a God-given purpose attached. The fulfilment of that purpose begins with the change from that unregenerated nature of the selfish flesh. That is a change which comes about by a process that can be very difficult to both explain and to understand because it takes us into the language of spiritual and non-spiritual experiences. These are polar opposites and no person can attend to get both of these experiences at one and the same time. Our physical birth leads to natural experiences through the flesh. It is the change to a deeper experience in the Spirit that believers express by the word regeneration. It amounts to the experience of a second start to life. This new birth experience will follow parallel stages of development, in ways similar to a baby who grows into maturity of faith.

Chapter Fifteen
Lusts and Desires In The Flesh

From the time that we are born on this earth we begin to develop an awareness of our self identity. We are given names, our first personalised possession. In the Old Testament Bible, we read about one being nation established directly by God for His own purpose. That nation was called 'Israel', and located in the the land of ancient Palestine. God revealed Himself as the sovereign owner of all the earth, and indicating that His interest must be above that of any individual.

It is the natural human style to place ourselves above everything, seen or unseen, and this is always an offence to the Creator God. We must always remember that the lifestyles and habits that we will develop naturally from the time we become self-conscious are not always the ways or habits that will please God. But though we cannot help being born into a nation or culture, we should become aware at some later point of things we will need to lay aside or change in order to live a life that will please God. The problem faced by every person is just how can you turn your mind from self and begin to focus upon the will of God. It is very hard to do.

I supposed the most natural pre-occupation in the chain of any normal young life will include those of new social relationships, sex, money and perhaps, marriage. The first two or three of these may come about naturally. But as for marriage, this would require a very different view of flesh and self. It is not an accident that at the very start of the Bible, Genesis, chapter 2, we hear God speak about love, marriage and reproduction. I think this was meant to tell us that God gave His approval to these activities, but that the order should begin with an understanding of love, and then marriage as a union between a man and a woman, and then the benefits and joy of sexual intimacy would be blessed. God also made it clear that where this order was followed, His own pleasures and purpose for our lives would be fulfilled. But I didn't quite walk along the route established by God and like many, I lived with a different order. I set about to please the desires of myself, in my flesh. I went down my own path for many years. So by the time I actually got around to marriage, my two beautiful girls had already been born. Marriage came afterwards. But I cannot honestly say that such a marriage was approved in heaven. It was not done according to God's will, or by His way, order or standard. That was inspired by a desire to satisfy the needs of self in the flesh. Those all the hallmarks for a future failure and that was what happened in the years later. Things fell apart quickly on grounds of marital unfaithfulness, dishonesty and adultery. My flesh and self said that I was a victim. The solution that came from living in flesh and self was to bring the marriage to an end. So I did just that to end that page of my life.

When things fall apart in our lives we will often look around to find ways and means to overcome and move on with life. I arrived at that place around 2009. During the next three years the pull towards returning to flesh and self, from where I had been, was very strong. It would have been quite easy to simply start over again with a new partner and get more children. But somehow, there was a quiet voice embedded in me that said, 'no, don't go back there.' Well, in some ways that was so much more easily said than done. Some things would just come naturally when you are propelled only by daily interest in work, children and family. Yet I must say that after some further years something in my heart would begin to change. That process began when I started to open my Bible again, and continued to do so more and more. I was perhaps seeking a new direction for myself. It has been said often that when the weight of the world begins to press you down the best refuge will be found in God. When I arrived at that place, the new air of being older and wiser became prominent. It is always easier to follow the crowd, as it were. But even after a while, I was able to stop myself and take a self-conscious change away from that path. A desire to repent was now springing up from deep down in my spirit.

Chapter Sixteen
A Change of Position And Place

Every person under the sun must come to a clear understanding that they are not indestructible, but perishable flesh. All must understand that God is a sovereign eternal Spirit, and is therefore not of flesh like ourselves. Each should understand just where they stand on this globe. God sits high on an exalted throne, above and beyond all of mankind. The very best of humanity cannot therefore be placed at the same level as God. That ought to be the most important fact in the life of every human being. When that understanding of the supreme might and power of God becomes clear and is accepted fully then all other areas of thinking or reasoning, planning and reorganising will also become adjusted accordingly. The proverbial one million dollar question then is just how does a true believer in God live a life that will honour and exalt His name? At the time that I ventured to re-enter the church of my childhood, the hope was to begin to give honour to God for who He is.

At its essence I understood that there was a earth based reference to the church which meant believers gathering together to give praise, thanksgiving and worship to God. But there was also a heaven based understanding that a church can exist without buildings because it comprised only the chosen of God. Such a heaven based church could well be made up of true and faithful believers from any congregation and from any place on the globe.

But in any case no church can hope to exist without understanding and accepting the Gospel of Jesus Christ and must be lead by the active presence of God's Holy Spirit. So if the church, so called, becomes equated to just a presence in a building or a name over a doorway, without the gathering and presence of the Holy Spirit, that would not really be God's church. It would therefore be a façade established by men, for men, and a counterfeit. Hence, the foundation of any place called a church must include and involve the abiding presence of the Holy Spirit. As a child I remember weekly utterances and claims from the pulpit that the New Testament Church was the House dedicated to God and I believed it to be so. So now I would return to the same church in the expectation that this was the best place from where to re-start a personal seeking and relationship with Jesus Christ, as my Lord and Saviour.

Admittance or re-admittance into Christian fellowship at the church would follow a series of steps like unto a ladder that would lead me into the very presence of God. Before climbing up the first rung I made it my due diligence to start reading passages from the Bible again. In the book of Genesis, I found one of the first impressions as to how a person might enter into heaven, the dwelling place of God. In this passage God had given a revelation to Jacob, the grandson of Abraham. This was given in a dream, in the twenty-eight chapter of Genesis. It happened that Jacob was in fact the second born of twins, but he had the greater consciousness and will to receive God's blessing than brother Esau. In time, he would find the way to deprive his brother of his first born birth right and inheritance.

(King James Version, Genesis 28:10-17):

10. And Jacob went out from Beer-Sheba, and went towards Haran.

11. And he lighted upon a certain place, and tarried there all night, because the sun set; and he took of the stones of that place, and lay down in that place to sleep.

12. And he dreamed, and behold a ladder set up on the earth, and the top of it reached to heaven; and behold the angels of God ascended and descended on it.

13. An behold, the Lord stood above it and said I am the Lord God of Abraham thy father, and the God of Isaac: the land whereon thou liest, To thee will I give it, and to thy seed.

14. And thy seed shall be as the dust of the earth, and thou shalt spread abroad to the West and to the East, and to the North, and to the South; and in thee and in thy seed shall all the families of the earth be blessed.

15. And, behold, I am with thee, and will keep thee in all places whither thou goest, and will bring thee again into this land; for I will not leave thee, until I have done that which I have spoken to thee of.

16. And Jacob awaked out of his sleep, and he said, surely, the Lord Is in this place; and I knew it not.

17. And he was afraid, and said, 'How dreadful is this place.' This is none other but the house of God, and this is the gate of heaven.

(King James Bible)

It could be said that in this dream God was showing al of humanity through Jacob, the gateway into His glorious kingdom.

The place for Jacob's dream, named Bethel, could be viewed as the gateway into the presence of God. There may be an impression that the believer must enter into heaven through a earth based church. So a right interpretation of that dream becomes important because the word, 'church', is not actually mentioned anywhere in the Old Testament Scriptures. It was not mentioned or revealed to the great leader Moses, the Old Testament prophets or the inspired psalmists. This is a fact that I would later find to be significant of itself. In the five opening books of the Bible written by Moses, there are many references to the children of Israel being, and separated onto God for His own purpose and called a 'congregation,' but they were never referred to as a church. Later on in the time of the prophets, references to the people as a congregation continued to be used in the Old Testament Scriptures.

God alone knows all things. His human creation was never given all the deeper mysteries of His thoughts and plan. Rightly, it was God Himself, in the incarnated flesh of Jesus, who made the first utterance of that word 'church', as recorded in the Gospel of St. Matthew, chapter 16, and verse 18. There was no suggestion that the church revealed by Jesus Christ to his disciples and New Testament generations thereafter amounted to being a earth based building or other physical structure. But what seems clear to me is that the identification of the church must be founded upon the Word of God, as uttered by Jesus to believers. So there can be no existence of any true church unless it was established on the true rock of Jesus's words and with the active gathering together of believers by the Holy Spirit. Today we see many buildings and structures with the name 'church' written on their sign boards. I have heard people speaking of 'their church' as if it could only be identified by a building. Others claim ownership of the church that they attend to the pastor. I know that such cannot be God's church. This is the reason why I do not subscribe to any perception that God's church is locked away behind the door of a building behind the name of any one denomination that is used on a Saturday or Sunday for meetings. In Jacob's vision of the ladder leading up to heaven, God showed us a glimpse of the heavenly church and the means through which to get there. The gateway would open only when Jacob submitted his will for his life unto God. It would later bring to pass God's plan in creating the twelve tribes of Israel through Jacob. That vision of Bethel can be interpreted as God giving humanity just a small mysterious passing glimpse of His future plan to lead us back into His glorious presence.

After some months of joining the congregation for meetings I accepted the invitation by the Holy Spirit working in me to join in a common fellowship and which was to be understood as the spiritual body of Jesus Christ. During the next years the essence of the Good News of the gospel message would become more clear to me. The Scriptures spoke about God as the Supreme

Creator of man and of all things, both seen and unseen. It also spoke to the godly moral commands that were given to guide the life of humanity into a path of love, honour and worship of Almighty God alone. But from the perfection of God's original creation humanity would soon fall away from daily obedience and fellowship with his Creator. According to the revelation in Scriptures, the introduction of sin came in the Garden of Eden, through the devilish figure of a serpent who would deceive the first man and woman with an empty promise that humans can be their own 'god', meaning they could sustain themselves in every earthly need. God alone is capable of sustaining all of creation and has set the moral boundary by which His human creation must walk and maintain to live eternally. The Scriptures use the word 'righteousness' to express the mode of living that will be approved by God in His relationship with man. In communicating with us, God has chosen words that speak to the state of a marital and family relationships. For example, God speaks against human tendencies towards unfaithfulness, disloyalty, adultery, idolatry and the breaking of vows. Such offences will always bring out the wrath of God with the most severe penalty in judgement and eternal condemnation.

Chapter Seventeen
Going Back to My Childhood Church

I had taken the decision to spend more time at my family home in Jamaica. In the process of time, I would also visit the church of my childhood. The building was still standing there in the very same spot it had occupied on the lower side of Riggan Hill since my earliest years. There had been some marked areas of building expansion with the original structure, as I recalled it. The original building was then set on a narrow rectangular foundation that was dug into a stony verge. If measured lengthwise from the time of my childhood, I would hazard a guess that the longest side then would measure around thirty feet. The measure today would be around twice that original length. There was one main single door entry originally but now double doors were positioned in the centre of the road facing the side of the building. A widened footpath now leads to concrete steps that slopes up to the small porch before the entry door. Outside of the door, towards the end of the building behind the pulpit, a prominent stone verge had been dug and then stopped, restricting further expansion beyond that point. Small offices occupied by the appointed pastor and the serving church clerk and treasurer filled the space left by the rocky buffer on one side of the building.

On the inside can be seen an arrangement of benches and chairs filling the space in the church. The raised pulpit remained close to its original central position. There were signs of other structural changes to windows and ceiling, and with electrical circuits supporting lights, fans, amplified speakers and microphones. None of these had been present during my childhood years at the church. A full seating capacity in my childhood might have been around sixty adults. Now the capacity would number around two hundred adults. Some of the faces I could still remember from Sister Patsy's Sunday school class. Those were now ranked with the mature members. Almost all of these had become parents and grandparents. Several males had always present and that was perhaps an unusual trend in this or any other church of a deep rural location. In many churches visited elsewhere the presence of youth and men in congregations was very rare to see. The love of God was still evident in the congregation I joined.

I can recall that during many previous visits to the district I could not quite sense a feel of home, but in the church I would again come to feel like I was at a place where I loved to be. I had no gift for mind readings and I never tried to do so. Yet, from the looks and faces present at those initial visits, the turning heads and lowered voices were familiar things. I did not always do well in matching up every face that I saw with names and nicknames from childhood recollection. Some of the men whom I remembered as boys, had now lost a little hair from the top or side of the head, while others had a thickening or sprinkling of grey. A few eye glasses were on view, with a toothy smile here and a toothy gap there. We had all been changed over the passing years in some natural physical way. There were some new faces in the congregation and even more new names with many of the girls of my childhood years now matured women living in family unions, marriage and re-marriages.

The structure in a New Testament Church of God reflects the teachings of servant leadership and on effective administration of the business of God. The first layer of support in the structure will be set by the appointment of a pastor as the spiritual leader of the local church congregation. The pastor would be appointed and posted by the Kingston based Island Office for the denomination. The office of my childhood church had been occupied by twenty-three previous appointees up to this point in time. Within this number there would have been pastors appointed and shared with another church, usually the 'District' church. This may have been the case with both the original Cascade district church and later, Sandy Bay district church. But in more recent times, perhaps more so since the 1990s, the direct appointment to Mount Pelier has become the norm and practice. The second layer is the office of the treasurer or clerk, who serve as the financial controller and administrator. Usually a spiritually mature and capable member, who is nominated by the pastor locally and made subject to the approval of the District Overseer at Sandy Bay. At a third layer can be found positions of deacons, or elected lay members to a church council board. These will usually be nominated by local members and their final confirmation made subject to the approval of the local pastor.

Ministry departments and support of members exist to ensure the effective service of the body, safeguards godly dignity, integrity, confidence and transparency for believers who must meet regularly in fellowship. The three main offices that lead and administer the operations of the church were still present. The King James Version of the Holy Bible remained the most visible book in the hands of worshippers, and this was carried alongside the New Testament Church of God Hymnal or songbook. The index listed the first line of 425 songs remained unchanged, with song number 1: "My soul living in sunlight, and

I'm going along". Then there was my very favourite hymn listed as number 2 and began with the first line: 'Satan led my Soul astray.' The chorus to this hymn is to me, one of the very best songs:

> Praise God I'm free
>
> I've been set free by the grace of God
>
> I'm free
>
> No more the path of sin I trod
>
> I'm free
>
> The blood has cleansed every sinful stain
>
> I'm freed by the grace of God,
>
> I'm free again.

We should always ask for help when we become aware that we are not free and have a need for assistance. I had begun to see my own need for salvation and I asked God for help. I had remained outside of Christian fellowship for a very long time. I was still emerging at this stage from my years of spiritual wilderness and I felt that it was in the will and purpose of God that I should maintain my attendance at this church.

Chapter Eighteen

Confessing Jesus Christ As Personal Saviour And Lord

I had attended church as a child without ever asking questions as to why we went there every Sunday. It was enough for me that the church was there; my mother went there and I was completely happy in going there also. The New Testament Church of God in our district of Mount Pelier has been a blessing to almost generations of local residents, to date, and is a tribute to its stable and reassuring presence up to this day. This also said much about the strong and enduring appetite in the community for the word and presence of God. Yet with all good assemblies or bodies, there must be clarity of purpose and a willingness to respond to people according to individual needs.

No one can hope to serve a master or lord well unless they first know what he is all about. During the age of the Old Testament God revealed Himself to Israel in a progressive way. They did not come to know Him, in glory, power and love in one day but rather years and over many generations. Yet even after such a long period the fullness of God's Majesty was not fully revealed and not understood, even by the teachers, lawyers, scribes and elders of the people in Israel. It is a lesson that we can never understand God in all His depth, detail and fullness because He is higher than we can ever hope to be. Yet God had chosen to reveal much about Himself so that we can understand love, trust and obey in faith. God is able to see all, hear and do as that He determines. He would bring to closure the Old Testament age under laws that condemned all transgressors. The rule of temple worship at Jerusalem and daily slaughter and sacrifices of animals to appease and cover over sin, would come to an end. All of God's promises of old were fulfilled in the Son, Jesus Christ, on the cross at Calvary, two thousand years ago.

Many people will probably agree today that the church exists to foster the clear and true understanding of God, the Person and Works of Jesus Christ. I therefore hold as true the often uttered phrase that all Christian believers must seek to know God for themselves. These words are much repeated and continue to be repeated around pulpits and among the weekly worshippers across the entire globe. I have heard this saying much during the almost seven years since returning to my childhood church and I have tried to pay heed to it in a personal and literal way. This is where any personal quest to come to know God really begins. As I make time to read through the Scriptures, with prayer and seeking after the help of the Holy Spirit, it has become clear to me that the plan and workings of God have moved forward, from Old Testament times and entered into the New Testament age. Perhaps the most significant thing in the entire Bible is the truth and reality that the same invisible God that we speak of today is one and the same God who was trusted, obeyed and followed by such Biblical figures as Moses, Noah, Abraham and David among so many others. That is as incredible as it is true. Today, the same words and promises of God stand before all people and in every nation, ageless, timeless, flawless, and eternal. It should be a great comfort to every human heart to seek to understand these eternal truths about God. This is also a challenge of faith that is built from within the heart of each person. It was the case that although God walked closely with the nation of Israel, protecting them and providing for their every need, many did not develop faith from within. In all its ways that nation was established by God and governed by the laws and words of the prophets. Today we can consider the fact that there is not a single nation on the globe that profess to be a theocracy or constituted entirely and completely upon the Word of God, the

Holy Bible. In point of fact many Islamic states are governed by the laws of the Koran. But in regard to predominant Christian nations, no person on this globe can be legally bound into seeking after God. The choice to seek out and to live in accordance with the Word of God must therefore, be entirely voluntary and personal. This is very important for me and for every other believer to understand.

By the standard of both our local cultures we have become familiar with the expression that, 'to see is to believe'. There is much truth in that expression, at least from the level of our common sense. Yet the things of God cannot be based on our common senses, but on the understanding of spiritual things also. No person can make the claim that their natural eyes have actually seen God as revealed in the Holy Bible. This truth has been the main source of doubts and questioning across generations past and present also. How then, can anyone say that God is real? I believe God choose to make Himself known to humanity, since He cannot be seen in a physical way. He has done so through the mouth of angels, prophets, the Word of Scripture and finally, through the life and works of Jesus Christ. Yet it was also in God's wisdom to know that without being seen, doubts and fears would overtake many. During the time of the generations, we read about in the Old Testament Scriptures there were many who spoke about God and some, like Nicodemus, were teachers of the Word of God. But as it turned out, teaching about God is one thing, but knowing Him is personally an entirely different matter. Very few people in any age or generation will actually come to know God in an intimate way. We read in the New Testament of leaders who had not walk in the Spirit of God and therefore, did not know Him. They had not experienced a new birth; they did not seek after the deeper things of God.

In every human culture it is also understood that one physically blind person cannot lead another. Jesus said that this was the equivalent spiritual state of many leaders in Israel. In such a case both the guide and the followers would likely fall into a ditch. This was in some ways similar to the leaders over God's people who did not know God personally and was therefore leading the people into errors. It was in order to free people from both further human errors and, from the bondage of Satan that God finally came to walk and live amongst us as flesh. Because by being present in the flesh God provided the perfect model as to how a righteous man in the New Testament age should see him, come to Him and worship Him. It was in His own supernatural power and will that God actually cast Himself before every human eye in the flesh of a human baby. In trying to understand the different manifestations of God, I picture the cast of a stage performance. We can understand that an actor can play several characters, even in a single stage performance. When we know the true identity of that actor, for example, whether they are male or female, then we should not become confused when they are cast to appear in different roles, even in the same performance. We understand when we see a male actor cast in the role of a female character on a stage. We know that he is just playing that role on the stage, and when the performance ends the actor returns to being who he really is. I think of God appearing before humanity in the likeness of flesh in a similar fashion. When we know just who God is then we should not become confused by His power to become transformed into the different personalities of a Father, Son or Holy Spirit. We should understand that God exists eternally as one God. Yet it was possible for God to cast Himself in human form in the person of Jesus, in Bethlehem, Judah, two thousand years ago.

God wanted to show humanity a perfect model of His own moral likeness. There was no phase in the human conception, development, growth or maturity that was missed by the miracle of the conception and physical incarnation in flesh of Jesus. He was born as a baby and lived in every likeness of flesh through every age and stage of life that is familiar to a human being. He came through a human family in Palestine, and a household completed with a human father figure, mother, brothers and sisters. He would have been known by relatives in a local network of grandparents, uncles, aunts and cousins. All of these experiences were real and Jesus certainly went through all of them. He would have been educated in the foundation of the ancient Palestinian religion, Judaism, through the Synagogue school in Nazareth. As the oldest male child in the family and under a watchful father figure, Jesus would have practised the carpentry trade of that father figure. After that father figure Joseph died, He would have worked to support the family as the oldest male and maintained the household. In keeping with the four thousand plus years of the ancient theocratic tradition, a young man would receive the call of God to enter into service as priest or prophet or other ministry, around the age of thirty. This was the norm for the nation and Jesus was called to begin public ministry at around that age.

It is important that this is understood clearly by every believer and perhaps new converts especially who seek to develop their understanding of the incredible love of God towards His human creation. It is only through the Person and Works of Jesus that we could be made to understand that truth. This further level of God revealing Himself to humanity through Jesus went far beyond what the Old Testament leaders, judges, kings and prophets understood. This deeper revelation of God came to us through the ministry of Jesus and not through John the Baptist. Jesus stood before men and declared plainly that He was, in all truth, the Messiah promised for their salvation. But the revelation of God coming to humanity in the form of incarnated flesh was too awesome and mind blowing for the very nation that had been so privileged in being established and instructed by God Himself. It was only a minority in that nation who came to confessed their belief of Jesus as the Son of God.

This therefore is the foundation of my personal acceptance of the God of the Holy Bible who I now profess to serve. As I read through the texts of the four gospel accounts in the New Testament, Saint Matthew through to Saint John, I can only try to understand just why the eternal plan of God included the coming of Jesus in the flesh. Because for one thing, the level of doubting and unbelief that Satan continued spread had reached its optimum stage of rejection against the Sovereign Creator. Yet God had always chosen and used human to speak to their fellow men, in relation to the truth and light of His Word. It was so with Moses, the judges and the prophets.

But in sending His Word, Jesus, in the likeness of incarnated flesh to the nation of Israel, in the first instance, and to the entire world thereafter, God had thereby chosen the time appointed to reveal His fullness in power and glory. This single act of bringing forth Jesus as the Anointed Christ and Saviour is perhaps the greatest mystery for a new believer to properly understand. Those having rule over the nation had lost touch with the voice and Spirit of the invisible God. The voice of God was not heard by His covenant people over a period of four hundred years, between the last prophet of the Old Testament period, Malachi, and the first New Testament prophet, John the

Baptist. It was this change in the method chosen by God to further His will and purpose for humanity that continue to be a puzzle and a wonder to so many. In the limits of the human mind, there have been many who refuse to accept that God would so reduce His eternal and awesome being into a tiny lump of human flesh. But I believe this to be completely true and speaks to the mind blowing love and wonder of the God to whom we offer up thanks, praise, honour and worship.

Today, our world is filled with competing denominations and churches and this makes it very difficult for many person to come to a clear understanding of the divine wonders in God. I accept completely that there has always been one eternal and sovereign God who established and reigns over the entire universe. He possesses all power, wisdom, knowledge and understanding, revealing Himself to humanity throughout the ages in the divine personalities as God the Father, God the Son and God the Holy Spirit.

A new convert to the Christian faith will get to know Jesus only by spending time in His precious holy Word. We get into His presence through hearing, reading, meditation, prayer, fasting, praise, worship and through the counsel of the Holy Spirit. There really is no other way to begin to get to know Jesus Christ. It is a great tragedy that so many professed Christians confuse the time they spend sitting in a congregation every Saturday or

Sunday with being in the presence of Jesus Christ. It is so often the case that what many have tended to call 'their church' is nothing more than congregations. The difference is that while any man or woman can congregate together in large numbers it is only God's Holy Spirit who has the authority and power to establish His church. So until that time appointed for Christ to return through the eastern sky in majesty, power and glory there will be many congregations across the earth. But there will only be one church called out in the rapture. There will not be any denominational earthly churches but only one heavenly church of God. So I believe that to sit in buildings that we call our church might not always amount to being in the presence of Jesus Christ. No building can provide that personal experience of coming to know Christ. We can experience His presence only through making our innermost temple clean to receive the Holy Spirit who indwells and fills our life with His grace and truth.

CHAPTER NINETEEN
Re-Baptized In Water

The Church of God at Cleveland, Tennessee is an internationally recognised religious body. It is under the broad Evangelical Pentecostal Christian umbrella. It is under the umbrella of that denomination that the New Testament Church of God in Jamaica, Cayman Islands and across the wider Caribbean can be located. It is the body which deliberates and declares the standard of faith, doctrines, rituals and ceremonial practices for all its churches. That International body have declared that water baptism by full immersion should be one of the first commitments made to begin the earthly march of faith unto eternal salvation. The act is regarded as an outward testimony that expresses the inward personal conviction experience. Water baptism by full immersion was endorsed by the four gospel writers, and they told us of how Jesus himself went down to John the Baptist in the River Jordan in order to fulfil the

Fathers will. But we learn that there are also further spiritual symbolism involved in the act of water baptism and of which I would become aware. In that single and seemingly simple act, Jesus had also taught something which other believers later imitated. It was the putting to death of his incarnated flesh before the resurrection unto eternal life with God that would follow. The flesh, meaning the submission of all of our self will, is left beneath the water. But thereafter, it was again raised up above the water. So the symbolism was that the rule of the sinful nature in a believer was thereby buried at baptism and a new nature in the Spirit of God emerged. This represented a newness of life and the point of spiritual regeneration or change of the natural born man. It begins a new attitude, behaviour, conduct, and mind-set by the transforming power of God's Holy Spirit. Hence, it is the normal practice in the church to offer this formula of baptism to all who repent their sins, in the name of the Father, and of the Son and, of the Holy Ghost. It was on this understanding that I accepted water baptism, and thereafter I was accepted back into the membership of the church. But water baptism should not be treated as a final step for salvation, only as the start of a new personal relationship with Jesus Christ as Saviour and Lord.

I understood this act of water baptism as my public testimony of a new spiritual birth that had started on the inside. After this was done, it felt like the Spirit of God had simply moved me to a new place in life. The narrow way unto that eternal salvation was only just beginning to become illuminated but there was no assurance as to how long or just how difficult it might become for me. In this public statement of a newness of life I also understood that I would need to be diligent and seek the face of Jesus Christ for myself, to submit myself, trust, obey and follow after Him. I would need to ensure that my belief and my daily walk by faith remain in total agreement. I had been cultured to understanding that a good earthly father would always take pleasure in the obedience of a son. I also came to believe that God is our heavenly Father, and that He brought forth an obedient Son who would do great works to fulfil the plan of the Father. That Son was named 'Jesus', and He was given a special mission to rescue humanity from the bond of devils, the pleasures of the world and from lusts in the flesh. The message of and the gospel is filled with the truth of God's love and mercy for fallen humanity. It tells of how our rescue from eternal condemnation was made possible, by the obedience of Jesus. The message of the gospel was presented to us from the mouth of Jesus and there can be no more reliable message delivered to humanity than the truth of God's unshakable and eternal love for His human creation. There can be barriers and resistance to sharing that deep love and these are present in the form of temptations by the seductive pleasures in the world and lusts that enter the heart through the eyes. I have been stained with guilt of disobedience and rebellion and was set on a path that would not lead me into a right relationship with God. Yet in His great mercy, God did not keep sinners like me under the weight of the law and where every transgression should be met by swift divine punishment. From the eternity past He had the full foreknowledge of the ways of human conduct and made the plan to rescue and save us from eternal condemnation, by His grace.

It is so often the case in our culture that whenever a free offer bearing great cash or other material gain is suddenly made to us, we get a flicker of doubt at the back of our mind. We may feel that way because in our nature, we believe that nothing which is good is free! Very few people expect to get something for nothing. But this is not how God relates to us. We receive undeserved favours and benefits to our lives each day because of His love. The gospel message is about God's great love for us and which results in Him accepting the sacrificial death of His Son on a cross to clear away all the sins of the world. It is a message that no human being should ever ignore or refuse to accept. Yet countless numbers have heard and rejected it. Maybe just the thought that God could be so generous in His love and mercy have caused many to step back in doubt. The message of the gospel challenges our hearts to recognize that we are all starting from a place of sin, beginning with our very conception in the flesh, and therefore unworthy to enter into the presence of a holy God.

Our salvation walk doesn't stop there with water baptism but continues with many further steps. After water baptism we will experience daily encounters with the presence of sin. These will come in the forms of people, places of evil doings, personal thoughts, ungodly actions and more. All of these will threaten to pull us back into sin. So we are challenged to recognise that we cannot simply separate ourselves from sin. We all need the help of God to keep us cleansed. God is aware that it is so and sent the Holy Spirit to help us through. Yet another challenge is that we must believe that God sent Jesus to lead us. This means that we must trust His Son completely as Lord and Saviour.

So the acceptance of the Gospel of Jesus Christ includes water baptism as the first step in that walk of faith. This is the gospel message that I understood and accepted when I went forward and accepted the immersion in water. The decision was actually made sometime during the close of the year 2015, and I had by that time spent much time in confession, repentance and prayers. I had resolved to restart my personal relationship with Christ. During a meeting with the local host pastor, at that time, I made clear that I had been baptised in the same church as a child but had not maintained a relationship with Christ. I asked about the process by which to return to Christian fellowship at the church. There were no more formalities of process except that I continue to attend meetings and to listen and read the Word of God. The decision was made by both myself and my wife to re-baptise and not least because she had also been baptised as a child in the Anglican Church. I continued at this point to read and meditate upon the Word of God, and do so prayerfully and in all diligence. I prayed more and began to develop some level of self-discipline for fasting and personal supplication. I purposed in my heart to focus daily upon the things of God. There were many former things and practices that I had done through the lusts of my flesh and eyes that would now be arrested and ended. Further conscious changes were being made at the levels of my body, soul and spirit. Many former friendships and associations would be ended. A hollow void was starting to develop inside. I prayed that it would become filled by God's Holy Spirit. I was beginning to feel a new spiritual presence of calm and peace inside of me each day.

CHAPTER TWENTY
A New Birth of The Spirit

I like to sing a personalised version of the Pentecostal chorus:

> *I have been born, born, born again*
> *Thank the Lord, I am born again*
> *Yes, born, born, born again*
> *Thank the Lord, I am born again*
> *Yes, I've been born of water, Spirit and Christ blood*
> *Thank the Lord, I am born again*
> *I've been born of water, Spirit and Christ blood*
> *Thank the Lord, I am born again*

I was now experiencing many changes to my daily life in the process of becoming a born-again Christian believer. I can best explain this transformation when I compare my present desire for the Lord with past desires to satisfy my flesh. There was now a daily struggle between the pull by my natural inclination to please the flesh and the push to avoid sin from my spirit. I was being moved to seek after a deeper conviction in Jesus Christ. Many things that I had been accustomed to doing, outside of the Spirit of God, I now resolved to avoid and to do them no more. There were words that I had been used to saying, outside of the Spirit of God, that I resolved to say no more. Many changes taking place in my heart had now to be reflected in the outward show of my attitude and behaviour.

A natural life begins with a physical birth, and a mother knows best just how painful the process can be. Women alone experience the pains and prongs from a physical birth. Thankfully, a baby does not suffer the same pain during delivery. The birth process can be long and laborious for some, while for others it will pass quite quickly and with only a relatively short time in labour. All said, it is by this process that every human, except Adam and Eve, has entered global earth and so we can all relate from our natural birth. When we think of Adam, we find the exception to this rule. But there is a further connection to Adam and that is the natural tendency present in his as it is in every other human flesh to seek to avoid future painful experiences. This is a natural instinct and very few will ever curb it. Yet in coming into a new relationship with Jesus Christ, the Spirit of God will demand that there must first be a painful cutting off or crucifixion of the ways of self life. There must be a willingness to put away many lifetime habits, styles and natural tendencies. It is a change process which begins in our inner being and will give start to a new spiritual creation. This new birth experience is all-together different to the physical birth that comes through the body of a woman. The Spirit rebirth may not be experienced by everyone, but only by those who are willing in their heart to crucify the rule of self-will over their life and placing the will of God first. That revelation and understanding of the working of God's Holy Spirit from the Scriptures becomes very important. It is from this source that we will encounter the spiritual gift of a new or second birth.

The Scriptures remind us that God is Spirit, meaning not possessing a physical body or likeness of flesh. For the natural man, spiritual things are neither easy to understand nor to be believed. As mere human, we are made of visible and destructible mass of flesh and therefore the opposite of spirit. Hence, those appointed to lead our congregations should therefore be aware of the great fascinations, fear and confusion surrounding the general matter of spirits in the world, and of God's Holy Spirit particularly. One of the clearest insights of the Spirit re-birth process in Scripture was presented in the Gospel of John, and in the third chapter, which brought that revelation to a ruling Jewish lawyer, named Nicodemus. He confessed that he understood the process of physical birth but not the re-birth in the Holy Spirit. This well-established teacher of God's law felt the need to make a secret visit to Jesus one night. Although Nicodemus appeared alone, he admitted that there were other leaders of the nation who have been observing the miracles and healing powers displayed through Jesus. Up to this point in time Jesus had performed a number of quite spectacular miracles in many places, giving healing and deliverance to the people and so perhaps Nicodemus and his colleagues were taking notes of all these. Yet Nicodemus and other religious leaders in Israel were not strangers to the public display of miracles and healing powers. After all they were Hebrew or Jewish and of the nation that God had chosen for a special covenant relationship. As God's people they were already believers of His supernatural powers. Nicodemus and his colleagues therefore had a strong sense of God's presence and power in the young man who had emerged suddenly before them from the small town of Nazareth, and known only as the son of Mary and 'father figure' Joseph, the carpenter.

There are some points that I believe to be important to my understanding of this late night encounter. Firstly, Nicodemus was identified as a Pharisee, so he was a member of the ruling class in Israel, and a religious leader. He held a position among the seventy-one Jews elected to the ruling Council, an ancient equivalent to a modern day party political executive body. Secondly, he was an established expert in the law, meaning that he had been schooled and trained in the interpretation and application of law or commandments of God, issued to Moses, for governing His people. Nicodemus was quite likely trained by senior religious leaders or Rabbis at the temple school. Thirdly, ancient Israel was the only nation formed and established by God, according to His promise to bless the seeds of Abraham, and the nation was among the most literate. They conducted weekly sabbath worship, and could read and recite God's law. They were always identified as a peculiar nation and were commanded to live by the moral codes of a theocratic or religious society. Fourthly, it was also likely that after completing his training, Nicodemus was employed as one of the teachers or instructors in the law and would have been involved in explaining the meaning of each portion of law, statute and precept for living in that nation. Fifthly, he would likely have taken a keen interest in the popular teaching and healing ministry of Jesus, from the time that He had first entered the Temple in Jerusalem from Nazareth, to begin three and a half years of public ministry throughout ancient Palestine. Sixth, the nation, Judah, was under the rule of the Gentile Roman Empire at the time of Jesus's birth and continued through His earthly lifetime. Julius Caesar headed the empire during that time and therefore, exercised political, economic and military authority over the entire ancient world. Seventh, the Jews were only authorised to rule over their internal religious affairs. Eighth, Jewish people were always recognized as a unique historic people of God, recognized even by their Gentile rulers such as in their time under the rule of Assyria, Babylon, Persia and Greece. Ninth, the Jews were not permitted to establish any independent military or economic bases under the Romans. Finally, they could only make their own people become legally subject to their religious laws. They could, for example, enforce the religious laws but could not carry out a death sentence, if they violated any of God's commandments. Also, they could conduct events of religious worship, animal sacrifices in their Temple, for ritual cleansing, and so forth.

Because of the nation's repeated state of sinfulness, God chose not to reveal the timing or presentation of His promised Son, their Messiah, to any of Israel's known rulers. Instead, this revelation was given to the parents of John the Baptist, a forerunner to the ministry of Jesus, and to the young virgin, Mary, with Joseph her future husband, a carpenter from Nazareth. After the miracle of conception and birth of Jesus, God then chose wise men from unnamed eastern countries and to shepherds feeding their flocks of sheep by night, to be the first to share in the glad tidings. When the religious doctrines or teachings by Jesus became known to the Jewish rulers they question his training and was angered by His popularity. They did not accept that He was conceived by the Holy Spirit of God, in the flesh of the Virgin Mary, and therefore the only begotten Son of God. So as Jesus established His ministry of teaching, healing, miracle and deliverance from the bondage and practice of sin the rulers would often send persons to secretly observe Him. These were like paid secret agents and they would then be charged to report back to the rulers about the things they heard from Jesus or from His disciples.

In a previous chapter, at St. John 1 and in verse 19, we were given a sense of this secret method of seeking and searching by the religious leaders in wanting to find out more about Jesus's identity and mission: *'And this is the record of John, when the Jews sent priests and Levites from Jerusalem to ask him, who art thou?'*

In verse 24, we are told further that, *'And they which were sent were of the Pharisee.'*

The majority of rulers were from the class of Pharisees and they became set against Jesus and especially His teachings that He came from God. Further in St. John, chapter 2:18-25, we get another clear impression of the heavy tension stoked up by the leading Pharisee in their questioning of Jesus's claim to be sent by God, His Father. Jesus knew the very heart and mind of all men, and knew the evil and ill-will of the leading Pharisee against Him. So, in their encounter Nicodemus would have been one of very few among their number prepared to give Jesus the benefit of any initial doubts. But he was clearly not prepared to let his personal sympathy be made known to the public or his ruling Pharisee party. So, hence the choice of a secret night time attempt to personally meet and question Jesus.

We could say from these observations of the Pharisees, that the Spirit to discern the mind of God was not given to them and therefore being spiritually blinded, they held a deep distrust of Jesus as the Messiah promised to their nation and the world. So they wanted to get rid of Him out of their blindness to God's will and way. Yet this one man was to be found among their number, likened to a remnant, who felt a burning desire to seek after the truth. At verse 2 in St. John, chapter 1, we heard Nicodemus addressing Jesus with genuine respect: *'Rabbi'* is a Greek word translation to mean a 'teacher'. From this address, we can see a sympathetic or perhaps curious enquiring heart revealed in Nicodemus. He continued as though a representative of the entire group when he said, *'We know that thou art a teacher come from God: For no man can do these miracles that thou doest, except God be with him." Further down at* verse 3 Jesus gave His first direct answer to Nicodemus. This begun with the repeated word, *Verily, Verily*. Jesus was attaching a strong emphasis upon the truth of what He was just about to say to Nicodemus. *'I say unto thee'* Here Jesus addressed Nicodemus with the full authority of His claim to also being in God and of God, without fear or favour. This is a straight and direct response. Jesus was looking deep into the soul of this spiritually dead teacher of God's people when He spoke the next life-changing word, *'Except'*. This is a word intended to mean that there was no other way or means; no exception to this need for a rebirth by the Holy Spirit.

The next words that followed, 'A man', and meaning any human being who developed a consciousness of themselves under the sun, under God the Creator. 'Must be *born again'*, perhaps carries the greatest importance in the entire passage. The very idea of a birth could mean only one thing to an ancient hearer at that point in time. Like the ancient Jews, today we also understood the word 'birth', to mean that of a physical experience following conception, foetal development up to nine months and then the delivery or birth. To the average hearer, a birth could happen only once to a human being. So this would mean then that Jesus's reference to the words, *'must be born again'*, could carry the implication of a 'second birth' or a repeat of that known physical process through a woman. That was totally unheard of by Nicodemus. Physically, this defied human comprehension, and going against the very laws of biology, physics and every physiological working of the human anatomy.

So having turned up with high praise for the teaching skills displayed by Jesus, and the miracles He had openly associated with God, Nicodemus's sense of reason would have exploded under the sheer weight of this declaration of the requirement for a re-birth. But Jesus was teaching him about birth again by the power of the Holy Spirit. Jesus had already insisted that there was no other means for this teacher of Israel to gain entry into the place where he clearly wanted to know more about: *'he cannot see the kingdom of God.'* So this Jewish ruler who was always teaching about God must have had a rude awakening. The re-birth was the non-negotiable condition for entry into God's kingdom, or what the Jews were taught to mean 'heaven'. Jesus had made a declaration which had a spiritual meaning and would require God's power in its fulfilment. Nicodemus' ears would have heard what we call a physical impossibility declared by Jesus. In the shattered state of his natural human thoughts, probably he could hardly bring himself to ask the next question, in reply. *'But How* (his voice perhaps stuttering, before continuing), can a fully grown man be *born* (again), *when he is old?'*

Nicodemus may have stumbled even further to say these next words: *'Can he re-enter the second time into his mother's womb and be born* (again)?'

It is noticeable that after this response, Nicodemus asked only one further question. This is at verse 9, *'Nicodemus answered and said unto him, 'How can these things be?'*

But I want to go back to verses 5-8: Because it was between those two enquiring questions from Nicodemus that Jesus expanded on a matter that was deeply spiritual, both in understanding and in its in actual doing. The entire life of a believing Jew was expected to culminate in their "seeing the kingdom of God," because this was in line with their descent from Abraham and therefore the fulfilment of God's promise of deliverance and salvation to his seeds. When Jesus spoke for the first time in verse 3, He started with the same repeated word as if to emphasise the spiritual truth and meaning. In verse 5. *'Verily, verily, I say unto thee, Except a man be born of water and of spirit he cannot enter into the kingdom of God.'*

But at this second time of responding, Jesus expounded upon the stark spiritual truth spoken previously when He said, *'except a man be born again.'* Jesus, at verse 5, added the words: *'of water and of Spirit.'* What then could Nicodemus interpret these words to mean? Jesus knew that Nicodemus would readily understand the process of physical birth. We have all experienced this and so can understand the 'watery' experience of the foetus leaving the womb. We also understand that water preserves life. So, it's also the water that covers and preserves the unborn foetus safely until the time of actual birth, which is when we leave the watery pool of the womb. The Spirit re-birth would therefore, come with the parallel experience of becoming immersed in the loving presence of God. The Holy

Spirit 's presence was to be understood in this way like the water of physical conception and the watery womb that preserves embryonic life. But this experience of the Spirit would not be like the natural elements. It is spiritual. Elsewhere in Scripture, Jesus spoke of Himself as being "the living water". When speaking to the Samaritan woman, He said that, 'Whosoever drinketh of this water (meaning to receive and retain His words and the indwelling presence of the Holy Spirit), shall never thirst again (John 4:13).

Nicodemus's transformation to a level of heightened spiritual awareness (his re-birth), could only begin when he believed, confessed and accepted Jesus as personal Saviour and Lord. So it is only when a heart becomes receptive to hear the Good News message of the gospel brought by Jesus, that God grant unto us a new birth, in the Spirit. Our new nature and condition, therefore becomes like a new conception. We get a second chance to begin our life again, but not physically. Nicodemus' body was not being subject to a new birth, but only his spirit. It is the spirit of the man or the nature of God that should now begin to rise above the former dominance of the flesh.

At the seventh verse (3:7), Jesus said to the bewildered teacher of Israel, *'Marvel not that I said unto thee, ye must be born again.'* In verse 8 He said, *'The wind bloweth where it listeth, and thou hearest the sound thereof, but canst not tell whence it cometh, and whether it goeth, so is every one that is born of the Spirit.'*

I think that these words teach us that no one can control the Holy Spirit except God. No one can direct the move of the Spirit except God. If God intends the Spirit to awaken Nicodemus, then that is what must happen. This was a very profound universal lesson to every Jew in Israel and further, as it was to every Greek, Roman and other nations. The teaching of this lesson by God, through Jesus, was clear and unmistaken. In order for a human being in this present age to enter into the kingdom or presence of God the things of the mortal flesh must first be shed or buried, put aside and replaced by the dominance of the Holy Spirit of God. That was the lesson that I believe Jesus was teaching through the meeting with Nicodemus. Jesus explained the meaning of being born again of the Spirit. With his final words in *verse 9. Nicodemus answered and said unto Him, how can these things be?*

At verse 10, *'Jesus answered and said unto him,' art thou a master of Israel, and knowest not these things'?*

So that lesson can be applied to all born-again Christian. It is a matter of personal responsibility that each will seek after a new birth in the Spirit. But we should also realise that it is God alone who can cause that rebirth to take place. It cannot be done by human self-will. Yet, that process to lead us to becoming renewed begins when we hear and accept the gospel message. It is from this point that the ministry of God's Holy Spirit will take us over and begin to lead us to the path of truth and righteousness. When we show a personal interest in knowing God then He will begin to respond to us, through His Holy Spirit, working from within to reset the condition of our heart and mind. It is then that our renewal and regeneration takes place. Just as the baptism in water wets and saturates the outside it is so that the pouring out of the Spirit will soak and saturate our inside. After a physical birth occurs we must then begin to grow, getting bigger and stronger daily until we get to a full size and physical maturity. There will also be a similar process of growth, development and daily maturing taking place within us after the new birth by the Spirit of God has occurred.

Other important things that will also accompany a successful and healthy new birth by the Spirit will be the quality and level of care and nurturing. In a similar way that a new born physical baby needs to be fed properly, and according to age and stage of life, the new born by the Spirit will also need to be nurtured and cared for in accordance to age and stage of growth and development. The digestive system in a new born baby will be immature and delicate at the earliest stage of development so it would go against every good sense to feed a new-born baby with complicated food or drink. It is a similar thing in the new-born child in the Spirit. The main source of food must be the

Word of God, but starting with the simplest, before progressing to deeper understanding of the things of God. The most needful early meal for a newborn of the Spirit will be in helping to know and understand just who is Jesus Christ.

Chapter Twenty-One
Restored to Christian Fellowship

The word 'fellowship', very often triggers a sense of two or more persons coming together for the sharing of something common, good and valued. At the very foundation of our Christian faith, believers in Jesus Christ were gathered together by the Holy Spirit of God. They worshipped, shared bread, gave thanks, walked and stayed together in oneness for the cause of the Good News Gospel. Hence, the public display of fellowship began with the universal belief in the risen Christ in Jerusalem two thousand years ago. This behaviour marked a clear departure from the hitherto unequal strata based, high and low esteem of Judaism which came from ancient Israel. At such a time when any new convert to Christianity enters into the membership of a church, usually after water baptism, they will likely look around their fellow congregants in expectation to find certain things. They may be looking for support, encouragement, guidance, acceptance or a warm show of welcome. In my case when I re-entered my childhood church after being away many years I did so with an expectation to find support for my renewed attitudes and lifestyle inside the church. I re-entered the membership of the church with my wife who had also joined me in re-baptism and we were both added to the congregation, during 2016. We both accepted that this moment represented a new beginning for us as we promised to seek after the new birth and to follow along a narrow path to Jesus Christ.

As I looked around it became apparent that some things had changed since my childhood while others had remained much the same. Quite naturally I was looking through eyes of flesh. I had not yet experienced the wringer of a spiritual transformation from within, in the way that God prepares those He gathers for service. I recall the popular homage of 'One God, One aim and One destiny', that was often repeated at the church building when I was a child. It was an expression of their shared belief, as encouraged by the Scriptures. When I began to read through the book of Acts, and especially the descriptions of the early days of the New Testament period, that same desire for oneness was very much evident among new converts. It would become the literal capstone upon which global brotherly love and Christian fellowship is built. The church had a long established set of procedures and protocols for admittance into its membership and these would follow after water baptism. In some way the process could be likened to the setting of a wedding ceremony where the bride and groom stand to face each other before making their vows. But in this case the newly baptised stand as one of the parties with the officiating minister standing in the place of the 'church' as the second party.

In accepting formally and publicly, the "Right Hand of Fellowship," was offered only after newly baptised converts were presented with the statement: 'You realize in presenting yourself for membership that you are assuming a solemn obligation, and it is expected that you will always be true to your promise and faithfully fulfil and discharge your obligation as a loyal member.'

Thereafter, you were required to give an answer of personal affirmation or rejection to a further series of questions, Firstly, *'Do you publicly confess and testify that you know the Lord Jesus Christ as your personal Saviour in the full pardon of your sins?'*

I do, was the answer given.

The second question followed, *'Are you willing to walk in the light of the Scriptures as it shines upon your path?'*

I am, was the response given.

The third question, *'Are you willing to abide by and subscribe to the discipline of the Church of God as outlined in the Scriptures?'*

I am, was the response.

The fourth question, *'Are you willing to support the church with your attendance and temporal means to the best of your ability as the Lord prospers you?'*

I am, was the response.

The fifth question, *'Do you agree to be subject to the counsel and admonition of those who are over you in the Lord?'*

I do, was the response.

At this point, the minister turns to the watching congregation and asks, *'If there be any member who has a legal objection to any of these becoming members of the Church of God, the objector may now state'.*

When no objection was tendered, the minister then proceeded by declaring, *'By the authority vested in me as a minister of the Church of God I take great pleasure in welcoming you into this membership and extending to you the right hand of fellowship.'*

With this declaration by the minister, the formal process was completed, and thereafter I would partake in full fellowship and the routine of weekly church services and in other activities. The menu of meetings remained familiar. Sunday was the main day for corporate worship, and these were scheduled routinely for morning and evening services. Monday for fasting; Wednesday evening for Bible Study and Friday evenings for youth fellowship. In addition to this menu, there were activities set by what is called 'auxiliaries,' meaning the separated ministries for women, men, youth, teens and by children. I quite naturally involved myself in additional activities with men. Local men have been well known to lead the work of maintenance and physical security and property upkeep. The actual organising of men, in an internal ministry structure, was led by a president and supported by a secretary/treasurer. That was a new experience for me. An organised choir of men to minister in song routinely had also been established. Here perhaps was an actual potential grain to benefit and strengthen fellowship within the local church. It is always reassuring to believers when they can see and feel that they are not walking the Christian journey alone. The fact that these acts of fellowship actually happened in our church gave strong indication that the members find benefits at these occasions.

Newly baptised or re-baptized converts such as myself, among others, must look inside the church for guidance in the ways of Christian conduct, daily living and so forth. It is quite natural that a new convert will take time to hear and begin to understand the Word of God. It is accepted in all walks of life that not everything that is heard will be understood and that the practical application of abiding by rules and instructions may not come easy to every Christian at the outset. The church is perhaps the only place that can make the claim to be positioned in the body of Christ. It makes claims to exist in a physical earthly form, but only in order to maintain the light of Jesus Christ in the darkness of the world. The resurrected and ascended Jesus promised to return and gather that body, the church, unto Himself. Christ is a Spiritual reality and therefore His church, must therefore become changed from a physical reality into a glorious Spiritual light. Otherwise, how would it fit in the body of Christ? God is Spirit and Christ is the transformed and glorified embodiment of the resurrected Jesus Christ. God had made Christ to become incarnated into a likeness of flesh, and named Him Jesus, meaning Saviour, so that He could be seen and followed as a model of godliness by believers. In His life and work on this earth He would draw people to Himself to share in fellowship. Jesus called everyone who would come into fellowship, and include fishermen, tax collectors, prostitutes, thieves, shepherds, doctors among many others. Hence, Christian fellowship is that display of our inner conviction that as believers the common aim is to enter into oneness in the body of Christ. It is the Holy Spirit Who leads the desire for fellowship rather than any selfish personal motive. So as new converts each must be nurtured in the body and offered godly advice and guidance. Where there may be need for clarity in the working of God in the life of new members it should be the more matured in the faith that should step forward to give counsel and fellowship. This is specially important when any new convert is seeking to be accepted as part of the family of God, in a church. In the ways of our natural family culture, the incoming convert should anticipate welcoming arms of fellowship. It is in meeting, sharing and worshipping together that a congregation will aspire and move in the will of God under the leading of the Holy Spirit.

Chapter Twenty-Two
Bringing Flesh Under Holy Spirit Control

Jesus proved himself to be the great exemplar for perfect righteousness, justice and truth. That flawless perfection was of a most obedient Son living in loving fellowship with His Most Holy Heavenly Father. In all His ways the Son remained subjected to the complete will of the Father. He acknowledged dependence upon the Father to supply all His earthly needs in prayer at the start of each new day. He was perfect in the understanding and application of God's Word. He was perfect in the exercise of faith.

The Scriptures encourage all true believers to imitate the life of Jesus, the author and finisher of the Christian faith. He certainly came in incarnated flesh so as to relate through daily living the experiences of humanity. At the end of His time on this earth He was perfectly justified to say that He overcame the lust in His flesh, the vanities of the world and the wiles of Satan. Such a perfect score card leaves me and all other Christian believers to face up to the ultimate question of whether any mere human being can today follow those perfect steps left behind by Jesus Christ from two thousand plus years ago.

My honest natural response is to say, no, I cannot do this as a mere lump of human flesh. I can achieve nothing that is worthy of God unless He enables and directs my steps. This is my understanding of who I am and who God the heavenly Father is in comparison. I am totally dependent on all good things and even the common air that I breathe in each moment of each day. God can readily shut off the supply of air just as easily as He can dry up every ocean and river of water. He is God, the creator of all and sovereign ruler over all things, living and inanimate such as great mountains and distant skies. Yet, instead of using all that awesome power against sinful humanity, God the Father has invited all flesh to enter into His heavenly courts to share His almighty power. Hence, rather than be worrying about being destroyed by a furious God, for all my past sins and transgressions against Him, I recognize from the Word of Scripture that I can be changed and that I can be saved. This is a very wonderful thing to me.

God has made many promises to His fallen human creation, and largely to encourage us to get up again and trust in Him. In essence, these speaks to the charge of either walking in His will and purpose and living eternally or, to disobey and fail to repent of your sins, then in which case I will be walking unto eternal condemnation. God's payback for unconfessed sin is a double dose of death, firstly our physical death, and then in the final judgement of all flesh, final eternal spiritual death. The understanding of physical death is completely familiar to all conscious human beings. The flesh of skin, bones and blood we know must someday die and be returned to the earth from where it had come as dust. But what is so much more difficult to understand is the death of the spirit in a person. The reference to the spirit inside us implies an inner consciousness in every human. The Scriptures bear witness to Jesus, shedding earthly flesh but committing the inner most spirit in His body of flesh into the hands of the Father. So we can likewise enter into His holy presence only in the return of our inner spirit in the flesh to God's Holy Spirit. A portion of God's Holy Spirit was poured out and made available in the world of flesh at Pentecost, two thousand years ago. He was given a ministry to begin our spiritual regeneration, by escaping from the power and dominance of the flesh's control. The new birth of a believer must therefore continue with the seeking after the abiding Holy Spirit. When He finds a worthy earthen vessel He will remain and indwell, bringing new strength and boldness such as was the case with Jesus's disciples following their baptism in the Spirit from the time of Pentecost. It was the strength promised to enable Christian service and in the years following the death, resurrection and ascension of Jesus Christ to the Father, every disciple was enabled to go out into the far reaches of the Roman dominated world to proclaim the Gospel of Jesus Christ as God's Anointed Messiah, Saviour and Lord. But such feats can be attained only under the leading of the Holy Spirit. The works of flesh cannot enable empowerment for Christian service. That power can come only from the Spirit of God. It is the enabling of the Holy Spirit which must suppress the power and influence of the flesh in the life of a believer. When the flesh is put under such control the believer will begin to experience a newness of strength in our life, and made able to do all things through the abiding Holy Spirit. Today, I believe Jesus Christ is seated at the right hand of the Father in heaven. The promise of Scripture is for a future in the presence of Jesus Christ, for those who believe. But He will not be seen again in the form of a baby in incarnated flesh.

Chapter Twenty-Three
Feeding The Spirit

The Bible is the most widely read book in the world. It is the heart of every true Christian church. It is opened in our local church for Sunday school, then for the day's devotion before Divine Worship and for preaching from the pulpit. The same Bible will again be on display during the week-days for fasting services, prayer meeting and Bible study. On the face of things, our churches would appear to be well yielded and grounded by exposure to the Word of God. The intake of that Word can be likened to 'good food'. There is always a great benefit from regular eating, and that is necessary to take in essential nourishment that sustains a healthy physical body. The old folk saying that 'we are what we eat' has certainly encouraged the habit for daily eating. This is also how I would begin to look at the need to have a daily intake of God's Word, to enable good spiritual health and strength to follow Jesus Christ, the righteousness of God. So professed believers in the earthly church will be presumed to occupy the highest position in righteousness, justice and truth unto God even as they await the Second advent of Christ.

The core business of the earthly church is to share the message of the gospel and spread around the good tidings of redemption unto salvation in Jesus Christ. The message should serve to remind us that in time past all stood as enemies of God, doubting His Word and rejecting His servants, prophets and messengers. The Scriptures declare that all have sinned and therefore a payment of death has been written in God's non-negotiable law. Yet, instead of sending judgement against offenders, God showed the deep and eternal love for His errant creation. In inviting confession and repentance God would provide one final chance to accept the Good News through the gospel that there still remained a way for humanity to become reconciled with the Father and Creator of all. A new relationship would be established under the eternal Lordship of God's only begotten Son, Jesus Christ. The time had come to present that Son to the world when the baby called Jesus in the Scriptures stepped onto the page of world history two thousand years ago in the town of Bethlehem.

I find it to be especially pointed that in several passages of the Bible the new convert or believer has been likened to a new born baby in the sight of God. As a new born, the baby will be dependent, innocent and always desire food, that is easily soluble and digestible. The comparison to the baby is fitting in so far as the Word of God is concerned with the food with which the new spiritual baby is fed. The stomach of a physical baby would not be fully developed to receive complex foods such as rice and peas and chicken. So that baby will be fed more easily digestible and nourishing milk at this earliest stage. But of course, the new baby cannot self-feed so must rely on the mother or carer for its food. It further goes without saying for every class and creed of human beings, that not every parent is a good parent. Not all will be attentive and patient or loving and kind to the dependent new baby. So healthy growth and development of the baby can certainly suffer and in which case it would give prompt to this question, 'Should the baby be blamed if it does not receive the right sort of daily food, or should the carer be blamed?'

Here we could use the analogy of shepherd and sheep. A good shepherd knows his purpose in tending the helpless sheep. He will always be minded to ensure that none of the flock is damaged, lost or left behind. When shown or led into pastures for feeding it is the shepherd who must guide the sheep into the best path and it is the sheep that must lower its mouth to graze.

Admittedly, there may be any number of good reasons why a sheep either can't or won't graze, even when the mouth is lowered. A good shepherd will seek to find out whatever is wrong with that sheep. Some shepherds are not so attentive at all. They take more interest in attending to their own personal or family affairs. They can be distracted from their task and unfortunately, there can be losses from the flock. As a new convert joining the flock I recognized that the best food for me to graze on was the Word of God and I wanted to lower my head and take in as much food of the Spirit as was available. I will always take the responsibility for things that I must do. A shepherd can do much to assist the path of the new convert in taking in God's Word. But even this conviction will depend upon the character of the shepherd. When in the service of God, each shepherd must seek first to walk upright before God, their master. Yet there are many shepherds who have knowingly departed from the righteous path of their master. They may not even bother to seek God's counsel each day, choosing instead to forge their own path. So as a convert to the Christian faith my Bible became a close companion. In time I would come to understand the need for the assistance of the Holy Spirit to help me to better graze on God's Word. I recognized that the Word of God before us was much the same as a teacher placing a book before a new class, to give instructions, to give directions in things to come. For example, from the Word of God we find clear and accurate revelation of things that we could never know about the beginning of the earth's creation, the origin and history of humanity, the spiritual character and presence of Satan among us and so forth. It is through the Word that we can recognize that although we were made of perishable flesh, we also had the moral likeness of God's spiritual character. The Word is our instruction manual intended to move us along, from one stage of growth in faith to another, from the awareness of weaknesses in the flesh to the dependence upon the sustaining of the Holy Spirit.

I began to read through the Scriptures more dutifully and prayerfully. Some difficult passages became much clearer to me over the months. I had begun with the gospel and letters of John, the apostle, and then I returned to the books of Moses in the Old Testament. I dwell for many weeks on the first book, Genesis. It seemed to me true that without the foundation of the Word of God presented in this first book, then so much of what followed would not or could never be properly understood by many new converts. God's Word have been given to tell humanity about themselves and to rescue us from Satan's bondage over the flesh. God has therefore used the Scriptures to focus on His relationship with the human creation and to illuminate the path unto the eternal destination He has set for each one of us. So it is by the Word that a new believer must come to develop a clear understanding of God, as the Father of all. This was one of the abiding truths that Jesus came in the flesh to proclaim to all of humanity on behalf of God. It is to me very noteworthy that no other teacher or wise men had ever presented God as a 'Father' figure, before the ministry of Jesus. In His teachings, Jesus shed light for the New Testament understanding of God. He was to be understood as 'Our Father, who art in heaven', rather than as a harsh and heavy handed whip wielder. He was a Spiritual Father to all, displaying all characteristics of a loving Father to His children. God was to be understood to be the Father who loved but would also discipline. He would continue in His obligations even when we become errant and disobedient, stiff necked and rebellious. The new converts would therefore need to grow with a clear understanding of their relationship and obligations to God the Father and this was perhaps the main duty of any and every church leader in the conversion, growth, development and maturity of a new convert. From the Scriptures it is the Holy Spirit who helps us to understand the eternal plan of the Father and the ministry of Jesus Christ. But God will never draw us by force into seats for learning. Hence, we are given the wonderful gifts of conviction, conscious awareness through our inner spirit, wisdom, knowledge and understanding, among other blessings, that we should apply from our earliest days in the church.

There are so many ways by which the Word in the Scriptures can be broken-down in the meetings of a church. For example, the pastor preaches every Sunday morning; Sunday school classes, fasting services, Prayer meetings, Bible study and a host of other forms of meetings are held routinely. In the normal course of a calendar year upwards of three hundred meetings will be hosted in a church building. Additionally, there may be meetings held in the open air on the street or under tents. Just imagine then the sheer number of meetings attended by a member who has been present in a church for say fifty years, or forty, thirty years and so forth. They would have heard the Word from Scriptures so many times. So when the Word is likened to a nourishing fruit that feeds body, soul and spirit, they should be made to be very healthy in the Lord. This is the great benefit from taking in the nutrients of God's Word daily. In a lifetime each of us will learn a lot of things with some of these profitable to our understanding of God. So, the Word of Scripture must be treated differently to any other source from where words originate. There is no other collection of words that speak of two roads to eternal life and eternal death in equal measure apart from the Holy Scriptures. There is no other collection of words that speak to faith and a reality of eternal life. None that speaks to a gracious plan of redemption for the disobedient, the errant or the wilful transgressor against the holy and righteous will of God.

The overall balance of the Scriptures speak to the revelation and completion of God's plan of human redemption, and this is set against a background of an appointed span of time and a certain final judgement that awaits all of us. The Word of God also speak to the eternal love of the Father when it teaches that 'all have sinned and fallen short of the glory of God'. Yet God still love us in a manner and fashion that we do not deserve or understand. In a practical way then, most believers might agree that our earthly church is charged with guiding us into deeper faith or belief in God. The true purpose of the earthly church should therefore be to guide professed believers to Jesus Christ, through the power of the Word and in the Holy Spirit. The Word of God indicates that every single human being who have walked under the sun on global earth will provoke His displeasure at some point because we have all sinned. We displease God by deviating even very slightly from the righteous path that He revealed to lead us into the glory of eternal life. Some deviations such as when a momentary thought of self-satisfied pride arouse in us may be said to be a very small offence or transgression. Hence, the very first understanding of sin therefore came from the idea that God made us for His own purpose or pleasure. We must note that we were not created to do or attend to our own personal interests solely. It is from this foundational understanding that we should be obedient and trusting of God.

The new converts' walk in Christianity begins therefore with the taking of small steps into deeper and deeper faith. They may start out very uncertain. But with daily devotion, trusting and believing the Word of God faith will grow, little by little. The hearing of God's Word of truth is the usual starting point and coupled with our understanding, becomes the first step towards a life transformed by the Spirit of God. So that clear understanding of the Word at the very get-go is of the utmost importance. Yet there are so many believers in our congregations even today who still need help and assistance daily to develop their understanding of the spiritual things and promises of God. In any seat or act of teaching and guidance in God's Word there needs to be a persistent seeking after the counsel of the Holy Spirit. I mean, in order to help somebody to begin to walk in the Christian faith, the revelations of God the Father through Jesus Christ, the Son, in the power of the Holy Spirit must be at the foundation to understanding. There should be no person who will devote a lifetime to attending our congregations and then to end up in the lake of hell's fire alongside Satan and other errant falling angels.

I will say in all truth, that the approach so often taken with a view to fulfilling this most crucial function of leading the believer into the righteous path of Jesus Christ may not always be yielding the desired harvest. Even so there have been ample opportunities to teach new converts from the written Word of

God and also, to preach in accordance with the truth set out in the Scriptures. So the full benefit in the Word of God is in the fruit of faith. It is planted by hearing, and then nourished by a clear understanding of the promise of the Christian hope in Christ. That hope may well be made clearer and also more meaningful when the awareness of God's voice through the Scriptures can be recognised. On the strength of taking in God's Word, both the shepherd and the sheep should be nourished. So if on this measure the shepherd was found to be ninety-five times more healthy than the flock, then a serious disparity exist. This must therefore mean that the flow of strength to the flock would be weak, with the shepherd retaining the lions share from feeding upon the Word. That disparity would be in need of an immediate shift with more attention paid to building up the weaker flock. It is the will of God that all His shepherds and their flocks come to hear and recognize the master's voice for themselves, and both are fed.

Chapter Twenty-Four
Worldly Forces Against The Church

Christian believers across the global earth share in the belief that everyone who yields to the call of Jesus Christ is special to God. The church is to be understood as that spiritual body formed under the headship of Jesus Christ, and it is to remain as the light in a world darkened with sin. The body must continue to inspire the saving work started by Christ, leading lost souls to rescue in the knowledge and love of God. We must believe that there will be a reward everlasting life to those who endures until the end of this age of saving grace. We know that in the world around us there can be found males and females, as God made us, and covering every age and stage in the cycle of life. So, the composition of the church as we understand it, should be similar, seeking out men and women, boys and girls, teens and youths and so forth for Christ. When this is the case the name of God will be glorified.

One of the common features of churches in both the major and smaller nations, is the steady and serious decline in membership and therefore, Christian fellowship, with adult men, youths and male teens in equal measure. This mirrors a wider trend towards disaffection by males in many other ways and walks of life in the Western world. At both home and abroad the trend is towards there being more homes without father figures, increasing numbers of teenaged boys entering prisons, penal and corrective institutions and increasing numbers of male youths living off their natural wits on streets.

In every local town and community the trend in males moving away from church membership also holds true. Yet it is in the power of the Holy Spirit that this can be stopped and reversed. Unlike the large impersonal towns and cities of Briton, many Jamaican families continue to have active contact with churches. Within many household or family circles there can be found professed believers, and most likely females, who will remain in membership and fellowship with a church. This is perhaps a crucial hook, as it were, with which to reconnect males to places of worship in our communities. In truth, the reality is that our females far outnumber males in churches at this time. We see a high number of our sisters in Christ staying on the inside while their husbands remain on the outside. Now just imagine the kind of evangelistic drive that could be put in place that begins with targeted evangelism for unsaved husbands to join with wives in the church? In the small congregation at my childhood church alone the number of unsaved husbands with their wives in the church has reached high double digit figures! This area of work will bear fruit through the Holy Spirit as He builds upon the Christian values that already exist in the homes of church wives, mothers and sisters.

The presence of men and boys in any fellowship is important. Due consideration of the areas of service rendered and any temporal or spiritual benefits forthcoming must also be weighted in order for men to feel fulfilled in their membership of churches. I recall from childhood that the work of building and general maintenance of the church was the traditional staple for men, youths and boys. But I do not recall any focus upon helping men to develop in spiritual or other areas such as in personal literacy, Bible reading, exhorting or leadership skills. In returning to membership of the church, I noted that there was now an area of ministry given over to men under the name of 'Life Builders'. This area of ministry would have been initiated by the national church and sought to bring together men in brotherhood for service and fellowship. This was a new area to me but the activities are largely familiar. Perhaps it was a case of there being a different label but in maintaining the same tradition of men as the workers outside with women leading praise and thanksgiving inside.

The Word of God must be the source of strength to all believers, sheep and shepherd and this is irrespective of gender, colour or nationality. Yet that strength can only become exercised by taking in the revelations of the Holy Spirit through the Scriptures. One of the questions that I often ask myself, is whether it has gone unnoticed that so many men in our rural community churches have not developed the ability to read the Word of God for themselves. Hence, the thought that if they cannot read and understand for themselves then they cannot begin to help their sons, grandsons or anyone else for that matter. I have certainly heard preachers belting out what appears to be mere cultural conjectures against the worldly lifestyles of men on the outside but failing to even alter the worldly mindset of congregants sitting right there in front of them! Perhaps this is another case which demonstrate that preaching at a pulpit, in and by itself, does not necessarily bring about any clearer understanding in believers. It really speaks to the need for other inlets to the Word of God in order to foster better understanding which can lead to the earnest seeking after the baptism of the Holy Spirit.

There is also the factor of such national cultural values that point men and boys into a direction of 'alpha male-ism'. The culture on most street teaches that 'a man is a man', and so he must walk, talk, fight and live in the style of a alpha man. But right there we will find a serious conflict emerging between the leading of world cultures and the leading of the Holy Spirit. Whereas a woman might not need to show or demonstrate much change in perception or place when she enters the membership of a church congregation, the man will often feel it is necessary to adjust his very identity. Just imagine for a minute that well known 'alpha man' in a community who has long resolved not to take orders from any woman. He then enters into the membership of a church. The church is seen as a place of order, submission and commands. Now let us agree also that his water baptism amounts only to a first step towards experiencing the fullness of God's grace in his life. In the time spent in the church before maturing in the Fruit of the Spirit there will be the need to nurture a newness of attitude towards those set over him in the Lord, and especially, obeying the many females who will likely be placed over him in every area of church activity. It is in areas such as this that future consideration must be given to the position and place of grown men entering the membership of our church. Because when the church environment resist the natural alpha ego of that man, youth or boy, they will certainly not remain there. Hence it is only the daily intake of the Word of God, in Scripture, that can begin to help that man to settle in the Holy Spirit rather than return to the familiar order and ways of the world.

CHAPTER TWENTY-FIVE
No Turning Back Into The World

In this closing chapter I want to give some focus upon three obstacles that lay ahead of myself, just as they are for every other new convert and babes in a church congregation. These familiar enemies are found in the world, in our flesh and in the wiles of Satan. Our journey unto salvation always begin with the hearing or reading of God's Word. The origin could be via any number of routes through which it first comes to us. In my case the Word of God was an ever present source in my family home, coming to me through my mother, and immediate family of church attending sisters and brothers. A copy of the Holy Bible was always present with a collection of old 33' and 78' sacred vinyl records and a battery powered radiogram tuned to preaching evangelists.

It is noteworthy that one aspect of the ministering of God's Holy Spirit is to bring together hearers to the Word. This is a mystery of God in that the unseen substance of the Holy Spirit moves just like the blowing wind with no flesh able to fathom or control him. So incredibly and, invisibly, the Spirit will do the work of testifying to the desire to walk the overcoming path. While the Holy Spirit is uniquely God, the flesh is uniquely worldly. It is the Holy Spirit who is the stronger and so the charge is for the will in the flesh to become submissive and obedient to His leading and counsel.

From the hearing of the Word both I and, am sure, every other hearer will be visited by the Holy Spirit's prompting and therefore must allow the free will of the heart to decide on whether to trust the truth of the Word or not. While many have heard about God and there are others who have heard personally from God, there remain many who will not believe nor trust God's Word. It might be a case that a hearer will choose not to believe the message that they heard or read, or maybe they just will not believe the source from which the message came. For example, today I am more aware of persons who have refused to believe the words that come from the mouth of some professed believers. You and I might feel a nagging need to ask them just why they would not believe the professed people of God? In truth, I have found that the answer often given to this question runs along the lines that far too many professed believers who shout and halla' (a Jamaican term for excessive shouting), the name of Jesus have not maintained any good personal testimony as an overcomer of sin. Many known preachers, for example, have not put what they preach into practice, neither in their own personal lives nor in their family. Local and far away scandals of uncovering the dishonesty, greed, corrupt and lustful preachers abound. Televisual media, print news and more so today, social media, will never be short on stories of such tragic impropriety by men and women who occupy pulpits. So this is a real issue facing all who profess to be living daily in accordance with the Word of God. Unrepentant ministers will continue to fail because they do not bring into harmony the things they say in the pulpit and the lifestyle they choose to lead.

I want to experience the sort of Christian living wherein the witness that I bear for Christ will always remain in perfect harmony with both the private and also the public life that I lead each day. Yet even after almost seven years I do confess that this ambition has a hollow ringing sound of the 'impossible' about it. In church we sing songs with words such as, "Don't turn back, don't turn back, once you make a start for heaven, don't turn back…" So from having made a start, or a restart with Christ as the case may be, we all face the challenge to stay on the narrow path unto an eternal salvation to the very end. I really believe that it is possible to keep on moving forward before Christ because today I understand better that God Himself has granted to each believer the power of His Spirit for this very purpose. In some moments of doubt and weakness many believers have asked the question of just why God gave approval for the Christian to be placed within harms' way of Satan. But this is not a question that I feel I can properly answer at this point in time, except to say that God possesses all wisdom beyond all of us. So since I believe that He knows all things and does all things for His own glory then I must believe that no believer will face more than they can bear. So we must walk in trust and obedience of His every Word.

What is more certain to me is that these three obstacles will continue to stand between us and the promise of an eternal salvation with God. As humans we are the very centrepiece of God's perfectly beautiful creation. The world is a big place and at times it gets overwhelming! According to the first book of the Holy Bible, God made human on the final working day of creation, before resting. Elsewhere in the Scriptures we have been told that men were made for the pleasure and glory of our creator. We are therefore His own possession. We rightly belong to Him. So if we profess to live according to God's will then we should be involved in joyful praise with worship and devotion each day. That is the sure sign that we know who we are and what our purpose is in the will of God. Yet even for those who have been members of churches for decades, they still cannot manage to offer up praise and thanksgiving each day. They cannot do this because there are powers and forces in the world that want to prevent our giving recognition to God as the Creator.

Jesus acknowledged the presence of Satan in the world before His twelve disciples. God the Father had appointed Satan, the fallen demonic angel, a period of time in which to tempt and reign over fallen humanity as the prince of darkness. So for that appointed period when Satan and his fallen demonic angels are allowed, they will seek to deceive and draw our love and affection away from God. This will continue up to the time when Christ is himself appointed to return and rule over a new heaven and a new earth. New converts can often feel they just cannot make it on this salvation road. But I give thanks to God that He has also made a way for each one of us who hear His Word and come to faith in Jesus Christ to continue on our path towards eternal salvation with Himself. So this is where the idea of the goodness of God to grant us grace each day becomes important to a new convert. Grace is about the power and protection given to each one of us by God to overcome our challenges. There is nothing impossible for God to do. He is over and above Satan and all the disobedient fallen angels. God is most certainly above all things in the earth and in the heavens. So God sees and knows all about human trials and testing and also about Satan's ability to entrap and ensnare us. God allow the testing of our faith to build up trust and obedience to His instructions. He also tests the love of our hearts for Him.

So in His eternal wisdom and loving kindness God always know what we need in our struggle with the forces of the world, and of the weaknesses of flesh and, against Satan. He give us the gifts of grace and protection in the power of the Holy Spirit. By these gifts we get the liberty to call upon Jesus at any time, night or day. Because it is in Jesus that we find all the armour that we need to ward off the move of these obstacles. These are firstly, the world, which lures us to love every material thing above God. Jesus made a way for us to understand the everlasting love of God, our heavenly Father. He paid the price for our past sins but did not choose to remove us from the daily presence of the temporary pleasures and vanities of the world. Secondly, the flesh, which appeals to our self desires and self will. But in Jesus we are led into the fullness of greater joy in the Lord each day. In Christ we have access to every spiritual blessings, with God able to sustain and keep us. Thirdly, the obstinate barrier that is Satan. When we struggle in a battle, the Holy Spirit ministers to us about the Person and atoning Works of Christ that renew our spiritual strength. When Satan employs his trick to accuse us before God we can go to Christ as our mediator and advocate, because He is seated at the right hand of the Father. When our past sins are held up by Satan to cause us to return to guilt and shame, we can go to Christ who has promised that upon our sincere repentance God our heavenly Father will not remember our past sins. It is in these assurances to us from God, and received by faith in His only begotten Son, Jesus Christ, that mercy is given and grace renewed each day. As a returning believer I have come to realise a need to ask God the Father for new portion of grace each day. I also know that God will always give grace to the humble, and never to those who are too proud to ask. So when I fail to ask for grace then that is the time when I will be at my weakest, and in such times I will likely fall back into sin. It is at such times when I am weak and cannot battle the world, flesh or Satan alone that I must call upon the power of God's grace through the Holy Spirit.

I close with one of my mother's favourite hymn songs.

I HAVE DECIDED TO FOLLOW JESUS

I have decided to follow Jesus;
I have decided to follow Jesus;
I have decided to follow Jesus;
No turning back, no turning back.

The world behind me, the cross before me;
The world behind me, the cross before me;
The world behind me, the cross before me;
No turning back, no turning back.

Though none go with me, still I will follow;
Though none go with me, still I will follow;
Though none go with me, still I will follow;
No turning back, no turning back.

My cross I'll carry, till I see Jesus;
My cross I'll carry, till I see Jesus;
My cross I'll carry, till I see Jesus;
No turning back, no turning back.

Will you decide now to follow Jesus?
Will you decide now to follow Jesus?
Will you decide now to follow Jesus?
No turning back, no turning back.

I pray God's richest blessings upon everyone that reads this testimony and then share it with others.

TABLE 1: PASTORS LEADING THE NEW TESTAMENT CHURCH OF GOD AT MOUNT PELIER

YEAR	FIRST NAME	SURNAME
1953 – 1959	MORTIMER	BLAIR
1959 –1962	WILBERT	BUCKNOR
1962 – 1963	WALTER	BURGESS
1963 – 1963	BRO.	HAUGHTON
1963 –1964	WILBERT	BUCKNOR
1964 – 1965	VANLEY	EARLE
1965 – 1966	D.O. DELBERT	BLAIR
1966 – 1968	DAVID	CHANDAN
1968 – 1970	RANDALL	CURNIFFE
1970 – 1970	KEITH	THOMPSON
1970 – 1972	D.O.	LEWIS
1972 – 1974	D.O. WELLESLEY	RHODEN
1974 – 1976	ROY	OWEN
1976 – 1978	CONROD	GRANT
1978 – 1981	ASHBOURN	ALLEN
1981 – 1983	WILBER	BUCKNOR
1983 –1984	VINCENT	LAWRENCE
1984 – 1988	DELROY	SMALL
1988 – 1990	LEON	RANDALL
1990 – 2003	D.O. CHARLIE	GRANT
2003 – 2007	NEVELLE	MALCOLM
2007 – 2016	BRADLEY	REID
2016 – PRESENT	O'NEIL	HAUGHTON

- D.O. (DISTRICT OVERSEER)

TABLE 2: DENOMINATIONS AND CHURCHES LOCATED IN MOUNT PELIER, 1920s – 2022

1920S	BAPTIST UNION CHURCH (SANDY BAY)
1940S	SOME HOUSE MEETINGS HELD AT MOUNT PELIER
1992	BAPTIST CHURCH BUILDING AT MOUNT PELIER
1940S	MARCHING PUKKUMANIA BAND
1950S	BANDS YARD/ZION CHURCH ESTABLISHED AT MOUNT PELIER
1950S	THE SEVENTH DAY ADVENTIST CHURCH AT SANDY BAY
2013	CHURCH MEETINGS AT MOUNT PELIER
1952	THE BIBLE CHURCH/
1953	CHURCH OF GOD OF PROPHECY
1953	NEW TESTAMENT CHURCH OF GOD
1976	CHURCH OF THE LIVING GOD (SABBATH)
1977	APOSTOLIC CHURCH
2014	THE ARC OF THE COVENANT MINISTRIES

TABLE 3:

PASTORS DEVELOPED WITHIN THE NEW TESTAMENT CHURCH AT MOUNT PELIER

1966	CANUTE H. RIGGAN	Bishop DELBERT BLAIR
1997	GLASFORD HUME	Bishop CHARLIE GRANT

About The Author

Almost seven years ago R. George Riggon became a born again Christian. He has experienced the goodness of God in his life and now seeks to encourage as many people as possible to thirst after the truth of God's Word and embrace the love of Jesus Christ in their lives each day. In this book he will share a new chapter in transformed life with you.

He is married and has two grown up daughters and a grandson in England.

www.marciampublishing.com

www.ingramcontent.com/pod-product-compliance
Lightning Source LLC
Chambersburg PA
CBHW041306110526
44590CB00028B/4261